P9-DXJ-496

T H E   B O O K   O F

DRESSINGS
&
MARINADES

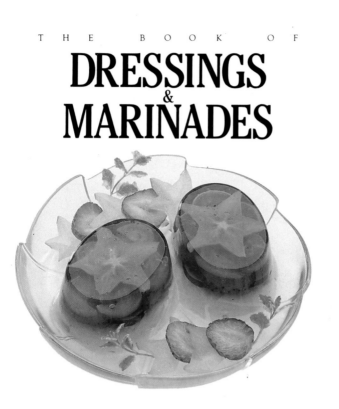

T H E   B O O K   O F

DRESSINGS
&
MARINADES

JANICE MURFITT

641.814 M975 bo
Murfitt, Janice.
The book of dressings &
marinades
3 1120 02237 1339

Photography by
Paul Grater

HPBooks
a division of
PRICE STERN SLOAN
Los Angeles

ANOTHER BEST SELLING VOLUME FROM HPBOOKS

HPBooks
A division of Price Stern Sloan, Inc.
360 North La Cienega Boulevard
Los Angeles, California 90048

9 8 7 6 5 4 3 2 1

By arrangement with Salamander Books Ltd., and Merehurst Press, London.

© Salamander Books Ltd., 1989

All rights reserved. No part of this publication may be reproduced, stored in a retrieval system or transmitted, in any form or by any means, electronic, mechanical, photocopying, recording or otherwise, without prior written permission of the publisher.

Notice: The information contained in this book is true and complete to the best of our knowledge. All recommendations are made without any guarantees on the part of the author or HPBooks. The author and publisher disclaim all liability in connection with the use of this information.

This book was created by Merehurst Limited.
Ferry House, 51-57 Lacy Rd. Putney, London, SW151PR
Designer: Roger Daniels
Home Economist: Janice Murfitt
Photographer: Paul Grater
Color separation by Kentscan Limited
Printed in Belgium by International Book Production

Library of Congress Cataloging-in-Publication Data

Murfitt, Janice.
    The book of dressings & marinades.

    Includes index.
    1. Salad dressing.   2. Marinades.   I. Title.
II. Title: Book of dressings and marinades.
TX 819.S27M87   1989   641.8'14   89-1810
ISBN 0-89586-819-9

CONTENTS

INTRODUCTION

Dressings are a mixture of aromatic ingredients, subtly blended as an accompaniment to enhance all kinds of fish, meat, vegetables and mixed salads.

Tart and tangy in flavor, they form an uncooked sauce which can transform everyday ingredients into a special occasion dish.

Different salads require different sorts of dressings, varying in consistency, texture, flavor and color. To make it easy to find the dressing you want, this cookbook divides dressings into chapters, grouping the various types together.

Marinades are similar to salad dressings in that they are used to add flavor, color and texture, but they are used primarily on foods being grilled, barbecued or roasted. They can also be used as meat tenderizers, glazes and sauces.

The marinades section of this book includes chapters on marinades for roasts and small cuts of meat, poultry, vegetables and fruit, all beautifully illustrated in color.

DRESSINGS

Translucent mixtures of oils, vinegars and herbs are always best suited to leaf salads, whereas the thicker, creamier dressings—using yogurt or cream—cling better to denser ingredients like avocados, artichokes or mixed bean salads.

Soft and cream cheeses form a thicker consistency when blended with other ingredients. These may be used as dips, served with a selection of crisp, fresh vegetables or fruits, or diluted with fruit juices or vinegars to make creamy dressings.

Fruit and vegetable dressings make a welcome change as they may be used to replace the tartness of vinegar and the richness of oils. They blend well with meat, fish, fruit and vegetable salads.

Mayonnaise is a luxury dressing or accompaniment to salads. Egg yolks, oil and flavorings are blended to produce a thick, rich, creamy dressing to mask meat or fish, coat vegetables, or serve with salads.

Oil
This is the most prominent ingredient in many salad dressings; not only is it the most expensive item in most dressings, but it varies greatly in quality, color, flavor and texture.

The natural choice for many salad dressings is olive oil and virgin olive oil (the oil collected from the first cold pressing of the olives) is the best. It has a strong flavor and rich color. However, the flavor is too intense to blend with delicately flavored ingredients.

Other oils which offer a choice of flavors, colors and textures are all the nut oils—almond, walnut, coconut, hazelnut and peanut.

The most subtle flavored and light textured oils are made from seeds—sunflower, sesame and grapeseed.

Vinegars
These are used to blend with oils, forming an emulsion and the base

for the dressings. They give added flavor and color. Available in a wide variety, the most popular choice for flavor and quality are the wine vinegars. These come as red, white or rosé, although again the quality depends on the type of wine used in their production.

They often have added ingredients to give more variety to flavor and color. Cider vinegar is often blended with honey, herbs and fruit and adds interesting flavor to dressings.

Yogurt and Cream Cheese

These come in a variety of textures, consistencies and flavors. Use Neufchâtel cheese, cream cheese and yogurt which are so versatile, being creamy but light in texture.

Fromage grais, being low in fat, is useful for a low-calorie dressing, Whipping cream, which produces thick, creamy dressings is suitable for dips.

Fruit and Vegetables

Grated peel and juice of fruits can be used to replace vinegars, giving a more subtle-flavored dressing. Pureed fruit or vegetables may replace oils and when blended with cream cheese or yogurt, give a dressing without the richness of oil.

Fresh Herbs

These are a must with most dressings as they impart natural freshness, color and flavor. Add a mixture of freshly chopped herbs to dressings just before serving.

Spices

These may be used to enhance the flavor of dressings. Saffron, in particular, imparts its wonderful color and delicate flavor. Mace, allspice, nutmeg and cloves are better selected during the winter months when fresh herbs are not so readily available.

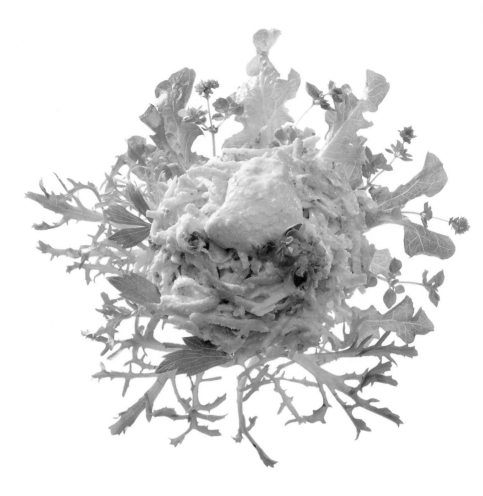

Almond Yogurt Dressing

1/3 cup ground almonds
2 garlic cloves, crushed
1/4 teaspoon salt
1/2 teaspoon black pepper
1 teaspoon grated lime peel
1/4 cup almond oil
2 tablespoons dry white wine
1/2 cup low-fat plain yogurt
2 teaspoons chopped fresh lovage
2 teaspoons chopped fresh oregano
2 teaspoons chopped fresh parsley

In a small bowl, combine ground almonds, garlic, salt, pepper, lime peel and almond oil with a wooden spoon. Beat in wine and yogurt until well blended. Cover with plastic wrap and refrigerate. Just before using, stir in chopped herbs. Makes 2/3 cup.

Variation: Substitute ground Brazil, pine or pistachio nuts for ground almonds.

Note: Serve with grated carrot and celery root salad, cooked green beans or rice and pasta salads containing meat or fish.

Coconut Lime Dressing

2 ozs. creamed coconut
2 tablespoons boiling water
1 teaspoon grated gingerroot
2 teaspoons finely grated lime peel
1 tablespoon fresh lime juice
1 teaspoon honey
1/4 cup plain yogurt

In a small bowl, cover coconut with boiling water. Stir until smooth. Cover and refrigerate until cold. Stir in gingerroot, lime peel and juice, honey and yogurt until well blended. Cover with plastic wrap and refrigerate until needed. Makes 2/3 cup.

Variation: Substitute lemon, orange or grapefruit peel and juice for lime peel and juice.

Note: Use to toss mixed fresh fruit salad or onion and potato salad.

Egg & Walnut Dressing

2 hard-cooked eggs, peeled, coarsely
  chopped
1 teaspoon light-brown sugar
1/4 teaspoon cayenne pepper
1 teaspoon Dijon-style mustard
1 teaspoon dry mustard powder
1/4 cup walnut oil
3 tablespoons cider vinegar
1/2 cup plain yogurt
1 tablespoon chopped walnuts

In a food processor fitted with a metal blade, process eggs until finely chopped. Or, using a wooden spoon, press eggs through a sieve set over a bowl. Add brown sugar, cayenne pepper, mustard, dry mustard and walnut oil and process until well blended. Stir in vinegar and beat until cloudy and slightly thick. Stir in yogurt and walnuts. Cover with plastic wrap and refrigerate until needed. Makes 2/3 cup.

Variation: Add 1 tablespoon plus 1 teaspoon of chopped mixed fresh herbs and substitute hazelnut oil and hazelnuts for walnut oil and walnuts.

Note: Serve this piquant dressing with fresh vegetables or hot or cold meat or fish dishes. Combine with cold rice or pasta as a base for a meat, fish or vegetable salad.

Orange Herb Yogurt Dressing

1 teaspoon finely grated orange peel
2 tablespoons fresh orange juice
1 garlic clove, crushed
1/4 cup sunflower oil
1/2 cup plain yogurt
2 teaspoons chopped fresh rosemary
2 teaspoons chopped fresh cilantro
2 teaspoons chopped fresh parsley

In a small bowl, beat orange peel and juice, garlic and sunflower oil with a wooden spoon until well blended. Stir in yogurt. Cover with plastic wrap and refrigerate. Just before using, stir in chopped herbs. Makes 2/3 cup.

Variation: Substitute lime, lemon or grapefruit peel and juice for orange peel and juice or raspberry, strawberry or currant juice for orange juice.

Note: This light dressing may be served with sliced beets or chopped cucumber, with potato and cooked vegetable salad or any curried dish.

Peppercorn Dressing

1 tablespoon plus 1 teaspoon hazelnut oil
1 teaspoon raspberry vinegar
1 teaspoon pink peppercorns, crushed
1 teaspoon superfine sugar
1/4 teaspoon salt
1/4 cup plain yogurt

In a small bowl, mix hazelnut oil, vinegar, peppercorns, sugar and salt with a wooden spoon until cloudy and slightly thick. Stir in yogurt. Cover with plastic wrap and refrigerate until needed. Makes 2/3 cup.

Variation: Add 1 tablespoon plus 1 teaspoon of chopped fresh mixed herbs such as parsley, thyme, sage, oregano and marjoram or 1 tablespoon plus 1 teaspoon of pickled vegetables such as onion, eggplant or cauliflower.

Note: Serve with grilled steak or fish, or use to toss a mixture of apples, nuts and celery or tomato, olive, bell pepper and onion salad.

Tomato & Olive Dressing

2 (4-oz.) tomatoes
1/4 teaspoon salt
1/2 teaspoon black pepper
1 teaspoon superfine sugar
1/4 cup plain yogurt
8 pitted black olives, chopped
1 tablespoon chopped fresh parsley
1 tablespoon chopped fresh chervil

Plunge tomatoes into boiling water 30 seconds. Pierce skins and peel. Cut tomatoes in half and remove seeds. In a food processor fitted with a metal blade, process tomatoes to a puree. Or, using a wooden spoon, press tomatoes through a sieve set over a bowl. Add salt, pepper, sugar and yogurt and process until well blended. Cover with plastic wrap and refrigerate. Just before using, stir in olives and herbs. Makes 2/3 cup.

Note: Serve with celery and apple salad, potato salad or cauliflower, broccoli and walnut salad.

Vinaigrette Dressing

1/4 teaspoon salt
1/2 teaspoon black pepper
1 teaspoon Dijon-style mustard
1 teaspoon superfine sugar
2/3 cup olive oil
2 tablespoons tarragon vinegar
2 tablespoons white wine vinegar

In a small bowl, whisk salt, pepper, mustard, sugar and olive oil until well blended. Whisk in tarragon and wine vinegar until cloudy and slightly thick. Cover with plastic wrap and refrigerate until needed. Makes 2/3 cup.

Variations: To prepare *Herbed Dressing*, add 2 teaspoons snipped fresh chives, 2 teaspoons chopped fresh parsley, 2 teaspoons chopped fresh marjoram and 1 garlic clove crushed.

To prepare *Lemon Dressing*, substitute 2 teaspoons honey for sugar and lemon juice for tarragon vinegar. Add 2 teaspoons grated lemon peel and 1 tablespoon chopped fresh lemon verbena.

To prepare *Garlic Dressing*, add 2 crushed garlic cloves, and 1 tablespoon chopped fresh parsley.

Herbed Vermouth Dressing

1/4 teaspoon dry mustard powder
1/4 teaspoon salt
1/2 teaspoon black pepper
1/2 teaspoon light-brown sugar
1/2 cup grapeseed oil
2 tablespoons sweet red or dry white
    vermouth
2 teaspoons chopped fresh purple basil
1 teaspoon chopped fresh hyssop or mint
1 teaspoon chopped fresh dill

In a small bowl, whisk dry mustard, salt, pepper, brown sugar and grapeseed oil until well blended. Add vermouth and whisk until cloudy and slightly thick. Cover with plastic wrap and refrigerate until needed. Just before using, stir in chopped herbs. Makes 2/3 cup.

Variations: Substitute elderflower wine for vermouth and 1 tablespoon plus 1 teaspoon elderflower heads for herbs.

Substitute mead for vermouth, 1 teaspoon honey for sugar and 1 tablespoon chopped fresh mint for herbs.

Note: Serve with mushroom, apple, nut and celery salad or marinate mushrooms or melon as a starter.

Honeyed Ginger Lime Dressing

2 teaspoons grated gingerroot
1 garlic clove, crushed
1/4 teaspoon salt
1/2 teaspoon black pepper
Finely grated peel 1 lime
2 teaspoons honey
1/2 cup grapeseed oil
2 tablespoons fresh lime juice
1 tablespoon chopped fresh cilantro

In a small bowl, mix gingerroot, garlic, salt, pepper, lime peel, honey and grapeseed oil with a wooden spoon until well mixed. Beat in lime juice until cloudy and slightly thick. Cover with plastic wrap and refrigerate until needed. Just before serving, stir in cilantro. Makes 2/3 cup.

Note: Use to serve with a mixed fish, mushroom and pepper salad or cooked mixed vegetables with chicken and ham.

Mint & Raspberry Dressing

2 tablespoon chopped fresh mint
1 tablespoon light-brown sugar
1 tablespoon boiling water
1/2 cup grapeseed oil
1/3 cup fresh raspberries
2 tablespoons raspberry vinegar
2 teaspoons pink peppercorns, crushed

In a small bowl, combine mint, brown sugar and boiling water. Stir until sugar has dissolved and refrigerate until cold. Stir in grapeseed oil with a wooden spoon until well blended. Using wooden spoon, press raspberries through a sieve set over a bowl so only seeds remain. Add raspberry puree to mint mixture. Beat in vinegar and peppercorns until evenly blended. Cover with plastic wrap and refrigerate until needed. Makes 2/3 cup.

Variations: Substitute loganberries, blackberries, strawberries, red currants or black currants for raspberries.

Note: Serve with any mixed salad ingredients such as artichokes, avocado, lamb, chicken or duck or salmon or trout salad.

—— Orange & Sesame Seed Dressing ——

1 teaspoon tarragon and thyme mustard
1/4 teaspoon salt
1/2 teaspoon black pepper
1 teaspoon finely grated orange peel
1/2 cup sesame oil
2 tablespoons fresh orange juice
1 tablespoon sesame seeds
1 tablespoon chopped fresh tarragon
2 teaspoons chopped fresh thyme

In a small bowl, whisk mustard, salt, pepper, orange peel and sesame oil until well blended. Whisk in orange juice and sesame seeds until mixture becomes cloudy and slightly thick. Cover with plastic wrap and refrigerate until needed. Just before serving, stir in chopped herbs. Makes 2/3 cup.

Variations: Substitute lemon, lime or grapefruit peel and juice for orange peel and juice.

Note: Serve with bitter leaf salad such as endive, radicchio and watercress.

Saffron & Pistachio Dressing

1 teaspoon saffron strands or good pinch
   powdered saffron
1 tablespoon boiling water
2 teaspoons honey
1/4 teaspoon salt
1/2 teaspoon black pepper
1/3 cup almond oil
2 teaspoons orange flower water
2 tablespoons white wine vinegar
1 tablespoon finely chopped pistachio
   nuts

In a small bowl, mix saffron, boiling water and honey until well blended. Refrigerate until cold. Whisk in salt, pepper and almond oil until evenly mixed. Whisk in orange flower water and vinegar until cloudy and slightly thick. Cover with plastic wrap and refrigerate until needed. Just before using, stir in nuts. Makes 2/3 cup.

Variations: Substitute pine nuts for pistachio nuts.

Note: Use with a pasta, rice, cabbage or green salad.

Sherry & Chili Dressing

1 shallot, finely chopped
1 teaspoon finely chopped red chili
  pepper
1 garlic clove, crushed
1 teaspoon light-brown sugar
1/4 teaspoon salt
1/2 teaspoon black pepper
1/2 cup olive oil
2 tablespoons sherry vinegar

In a small bowl, mix shallot, chili pepper, garlic, brown sugar, salt, pepper and olive oil with a wooden spoon. Beat in vinegar until mixture becomes cloudy and evenly blended. Cover with plastic wrap and refrigerate until needed. Makes 2/3 cup.

Variations:
Substitute 1 tablespoon plus 1 teaspoon chopped red or yellow bell pepper for red chili pepper.

Note: Serve with a mixed bean salad such as kidney, lima beans, navy beans and black beans, hard-cooked eggs and garbanzo beans or mixed salad ingredients and tuna fish.

Spiced Bitters Dressing

1/4 teaspoon salt
1/2 teaspoon black pepper
1/2 teaspoon Dijon-style mustard
1 teaspoon superfine sugar
2 teaspoons allspice berries, crushed
1/2 cup peanut oil
1 tablespoon angostura bitters
2 tablespoons red wine vinegar

In a small bowl, whisk salt, pepper, mustard, sugar, allspice berries and peanut oil until evenly blended. Whisk in bitters and vinegar until mixture becomes cloudy and slightly thick. Cover with plastic wrap and refrigerate until needed. Makes 2/3 cup.

Variations: Add 1 tablespoon plus 1 teaspoon of chopped fresh mixed herbs.

Note: Serve with a mixed green salad using red or green leaf lettuce, romaine lettuce, curly endive and chicory or a Caesar Salad with anchovies, crispy bread cubes, garlic and Parmesan cheese.

Sunset Dressing

1/4 teaspoon salt
1/2 teaspoon black pepper
1 teaspoon Dijon-style mustard
1/2 cup grapeseed oil
1 tablespoon plus 1 teaspoon Grenadine
 syrup
2 tablespoons black currant wine vinegar
2 tablespoons chopped fresh basil

In a small bowl, whisk salt, pepper, mustard and grapeseed oil until well mixed. Whisk in Grenadine syrup and vinegar until mixture is well blended. Stir in basil. Cover with plastic wrap and refrigerate until needed. Dressing will separate in several layers from pale yellow to deep red with herbs suspended in middle. Stir before using. Makes 2/3 cup.

Variations:
Substitute raspberry vinegar for black currant vinegar and raspberries for basil.

Note: Use for mixed salad of all kinds. This is especially good with avocado and orange salad or cold meat and Jerusalem artichokes.

Sweet & Sour Dressing

1/4 yellow bell pepper
1/4 red bell pepper
1 shallot, finely chopped
1 garlic clove, crushed
1/4 teaspoon salt
1/2 teaspoon black pepper
1/2 teaspoon paprika
2 teaspoons prepared mustard
1 tablespoon plus 1 teaspoon light-brown
   sugar
1 teaspoon Worcestershire sauce
1 tablespoon tomato paste
1/2 cup olive oil
1/3 cup black currant vinegar

Preheat oven to 400F (205C). Bake peppers, skin side up, in pre-heated oven until skin is charred. Peel and chop peppers finely. Refrigerate until cold. Meanwhile, in a small bowl, beat shallot, garlic, salt, pepper, paprika, mustard, brown sugar, Worcestershire sauce, tomato paste and olive oil with a wooden spoon until well blended. Beat in vinegar until mixture becomes cloudy and slightly thick. Stir in cold peppers until well blended. Cover with plastic wrap and refrigerate until needed. Makes 2/3 cup.

Note: Serve with mixed rice salad or cabbage, apple and onion coleslaw.

Grapefruit Ginger Dressing

1/4 teaspoon salt
1/4 teaspoon black pepper
1/4 teaspoon dry mustard powder
2 teaspoons finely grated grapefruit peel
1/2 cup almond oil
2 tablespoons ginger wine
2 tablespoons fresh grapefruit juice

In a small bowl, mix salt, pepper, dry mustard, grapefruit peel and almond oil with a wooden spoon until well blended. Beat in wine and grapefruit juice until cloudy and slightly thick. Cover with plastic wrap and refrigerate until needed. Whisk before serving.

Variations: Substitute orange, lemon or lime peel and juice for grapefruit peel and juice. Add 1 tablespoon plus 1 teaspoon of chopped fresh mint or rosemary to give added flavor and color.

Note: Serve with a red cabbage and apple salad or beet and celery salad.

Walnut Dressing

1 teaspoon light-brown sugar
1 teaspoon Dijon-style mustard
1/4 teaspoon salt
1/2 teaspoon black pepper
1/2 cup walnut oil
2 tablespoons cider vinegar
1 tablespoon finely chopped walnuts
1 tablespoon chopped fresh sage

In a small bowl, whisk brown sugar, mustard, salt, pepper and walnut oil until well blended. Whisk in vinegar until cloudy and slightly thick. Cover with plastic wrap and refrigerate until needed. Just before using, stir in walnuts and sage. Makes 2/3 cup.

Variations: Substitute peanut oil and peanuts, almond oil and almonds or hazelnut oil and hazelnuts for walnut oil and walnuts.

Note: Serve with a pasta salad and bell peppers.

Celery Fennel Dressing

1/3 cup grated celery root
1 tablespoon chopped green onion
2 tablespoons chopped fennel bulb
1 tablespoon chopped fennel leaves
1/4 teaspoon salt
1/2 teaspoon black pepper
1/4 teaspoon dry mustard powder
1 teaspoon honey
2 tablespoons green peppercorn vinegar
2/3 cup dairy sour cream

In a medium-size bowl, combine celery root, green onion, fennel bulb and leaves, salt, pepper, dry mustard and honey with a wooden spoon. Stir in vinegar and sour cream until all ingredients are well blended. Cover with plastic wrap and refrigerate until needed. Makes 1-1/2 cups.

Variation: Substitute 2 tablespoons grated horseradish or extra strong horseradish sauce for celery root.

Note: Serve with cold meats or fish, potato and bacon salad, mixed bean and garbanzo bean salad or cold pasta.

Creamy Eggplant Dressing

1 (10-oz.) eggplant
1 garlic clove, crushed
1/4 teaspoon cayenne pepper
1/4 teaspoon salt
1/4 teaspoon dry mustard powder
2/3 cup dairy sour cream
1 tablespoon plus 1 teaspoon chopped
    fresh cilantro or tarragon

Preheat oven to 400F (205C). Bake eggplant, turning occasionally, in preheated oven 15 to 20 minutes or until skin has charred and flesh is soft. Cool slightly and peel. In a food processor fitted with a metal blade, process eggplant to a puree. Or, using a wooden spoon, press eggplant through a sieve set over a bowl. Add garlic, cayenne pepper, salt, dry mustard and sour cream and process until smooth. Pour dressing into a small bowl. Cover with plastic wrap and refrigerate until needed. Just before using, stir in cilantro. Makes about 1-1/2 cups.

Note: Use this dressing as a dip with fresh vegetables or as a dressing to accompany all types of salads. Being creamy in texture, it is good for coating new potatoes, cooked mixed vegetables, hard-cooked eggs and chunks of tuna.

Dill & Cucumber Dressing

1 (2-inch) piece cucumber, peeled
1/4 teaspoon salt
1 tablespoon chopped fresh dill weed
2 teaspoons snipped fresh chives
1/4 teaspoon paprika
1 teaspoon finely grated orange peel
1 tablespoon fresh orange juice
2/3 cup dairy sour cream

Cut cucumber in 1/4-inch dice. Place in a small bowl and sprinkle with salt. Refrigerate 30 minutes. Meanwhile, in a small bowl, mix dill weed, chives, paprika, orange peel and juice and sour cream with a wooden spoon until evenly blended. Cover with plastic wrap and refrigerate. Drain cucumber. Pat dry on paper towels. Stir into sour-cream mixture. Cover with plastic wrap and refrigerate until needed. Makes 2/3 cup.

Variation: Substitute chopped fresh mint, thyme or basil for dill weed.

Note: Serve with potato salad or cold mixed cooked vegetables such as cauliflower, brocolli, cucumber, beans and peas.

Lentil Dressing

1-1/4 cups water
1/3 cup red lentils
1/4 teaspoon salt
1/2 teaspoon black pepper
1/4 teaspoon ground nutmeg
1 tablespoon snipped fresh chives
2/3 cup dairy sour cream

Bring water to a boil in a small saucepan. Place lentils in boiling water, cover and simmer 20 minutes or until all water has been absorbed. In a food processor fitted with a metal blade, process lentils to a puree. Or, using a wooden spoon, press lentils through a fine sieve set over a bowl. Add salt, pepper, nutmeg, chives and sour cream and process a few seconds until evenly blended. Pour dressing into a small bowl. Cover with plastic wrap and refrigerate until needed. Makes 2/3 cup.

Variation: For a thinner dressing, add fresh orange juice or use vinegar for a sharper flavor.

Note: Serve with hard-cooked eggs and stuffed green olives.

—————— Apple & Madeira Dressing ——————

1 (10-oz.) apple, peeled, cored, grated
1/3 cup water
1 teaspoon light-brown sugar
1/3 cup sunflower oil
1/4 cup Madeira wine

In a small saucepan, combine apple and water. Bring to a boil. Simmer until tender. In a food processor fitted with a metal blade, process apple and liquid to a puree. Or, using a wooden spoon, press apple and liquid through a sieve set over a bowl. Transfer puree to a small bowl and stir in brown sugar. Refrigerate until cold. Beat in sunflower oil and wine until well blended. Cover with plastic wrap and refrigerate until needed. Makes 1 cup.

Note: Serve with cold pork and rice salad, mixed pasta, hot pork, poultry or game birds.

Cherry Cinnamon Dressing

1 cup fresh sweet cherries, pitted
1/3 cup rosé wine
1/4 teaspoon ground cinnamon
1 teaspoon superfine sugar
1/3 cup poppyseed oil

In a small saucepan, combine cherries, wine and cinnamon. Bring to a boil. Cover and simmer 2 to 3 minutes or until cherries are tender. In a food processor fitted with a metal blade, process cherries and liquid to a puree. Or, using a wooden spoon, press cherries and liquid through a sieve set over a bowl. Add sugar and poppyseed oil and process until thick and smooth. Cover with plastic wrap and refrigerate until needed. Makes 2/3 cup.

Note: Serve with cold duck, hot poultry or game, goose or pheasant salad, or apple, celery, nut and bell pepper salad.

—— Cranberry & Orange Dressing ——

3/4 cup cranberries
1/3 cup fresh orange juice
2 teaspoons finely grated orange peel
1 tablespoon honey
1/4 cup peanut oil
1/2 teaspoon ground cinnamon
1 tablespoon red wine vinegar

In a small saucepan, bring cranberries and orange juice to a boil. Cover and simmer until cranberries are tender. In a food processor fitted with a metal blade, process cranberries and liquid to a puree. Or, using a wooden spoon, press cranberries and liquid through a sieve set over a bowl. Add orange peel, honey, peanut oil and cinnamon and process until thick and smooth. Stir in vinegar until well blended. Cover with plastic wrap and refrigerate until needed. Makes 1 cup.

Note: Serve as an accompaniment to roast turkey, goose, duck or game birds. Serve also with cold poultry or game salads and pâtés.

Gooseberry & Mint Dressing

2/3 cup gooseberries
2 tablespoons water
2 tablespoons superfine sugar
2 tablespoons chopped fresh mint
1/2 teaspoon grated nutmeg
1/3 cup olive oil
2 tablespoons cottage cheese, sieved

In a small saucepan, bring gooseberries and water to a boil. Cover and simmer 3 to 4 minutes or until gooseberries are tender. Using a wooden spoon, press gooseberries and liquid through a sieve set over a bowl. Stir sugar, mint and nutmeg into gooseberry puree. Refrigerate until cold. Beat oil into puree until evenly blended and thick. Stir in cottage cheese until smooth. Cover with plastic wrap and refrigerate until needed. Makes 1 cup.

Note: Serve with grilled mackerel or trout pâté. Use to toss green salad or cabbage, apple, celery and onion salad.

—— Pomegranate & Melon Dressing ——

1 pomegranate, peeled, seeded
1/2 Ogen melon, seeded
2 teaspoons finely grated lime peel
1 tablespoon lime juice
1/2 teaspoon ground mace
1 tablespoon chopped fresh lemon
1/2 teaspoon chopped fresh thyme

Using a wooden spoon, press pomegranate through a sieve set over a bowl. Using wooden spoon, press melon through sieve into pomegranante juice. Stir in lime peel and juice, mace, lemon and thyme until well blended. Cover with plastic wrap and refrigerate until needed. Makes 1 cup.

Note: Serve with fresh fruit, fruit salad, green salad or fish dishes.

Tropical Dressing

1 mango, peeled
2 passion fruit, cut in half, seeded
1 teaspoon grated gingerroot
1/3 cup almond oil
2 tablespoons black currant vinegar
1 tablespoon chopped fresh borage

Cut mango flesh away from pit. Using a wooden spoon, press flesh through a sieve set over a bowl. Scoop out passion fruit flesh into sieve. Using wooden spoon, press flesh through sieve into mango juice until only seeds remain. Beat in gingerroot and almond oil until thick. Stir in vinegar and borage until well blended. Cover with plastic wrap and refrigerate until needed. Makes 1 cup.

Note: Serve with fresh fruit, fruit salad, curry dishes, poultry or fish.

Gazpacho Dressing

2 tomatoes, peeled, seeded, chopped
1-1/2 cups soft bread crumbs
1/4 cup sherry vinegar
1/3 cup olive oil
1 tablespoon finely chopped shallots
1 tablespoon finely chopped red bell
   pepper
1 tablespoon finely chopped green bell
   pepper
1 (2-inch) piece cucumber, peeled, finely
   chopped
2 teaspoons chili sauce
1/4 teaspoon salt
1/2 teaspoon black pepper
1 teaspoon Dijon-style mustard

In a food processor fitted with a metal blade, process all ingredients to a puree. Or, in a small bowl, beat tomatoes, bread crumbs, vinegar and oil until well blended. Add shallots, bell peppers, cucumber, chili sauce, salt, pepper and mustard and mix until well blended. Cover with plastic wrap and refrigerate until needed. Makes 1 cup.

Note: Serve with Salad Niçoise with peppers, onions, olives, anchovies, beans, eggs and tomatoes or serve with a mixed vegetable or green salad.

Green Lentil Dressing

1/3 cup green lentils, soaked overnight
1-1/4 cups boiling water
1/2 teaspoon salt
1/2 teaspoon black pepper
1 garlic clove
1 tablespoon grated onion
1/2 green chili pepper, chopped
1 tablespoon chopped fresh parsley
1/3 cup hazelnut oil
1/4 cup dairy sour cream

In a small saucepan, cook lentils in boiling water 20 minutes or until all water has been absorbed. In a food processor fitted with a metal blade, process lentils, salt, pepper, garlic, onion, chili pepper, parsley and hazelnut oil to a puree. Add sour cream and process until smooth and creamy. Cover with plastic wrap and refrigerate until needed. Makes 1 cup.

Note: Serve as an accompaniment to fresh vegetables, use to toss potato or vegetable salad or serve as a dip.

Bell Pepper Dressing

2 (4-oz.) green bell peppers
1 garlic clove, crushed
1 teaspoon paprika
1/4 teaspoon salt
1/4 teaspoon black pepper
1/2 teaspoon dry mustard powder
1/2 cup olive oil
1 tablespoon raspberry vinegar

Preheat oven to 400F (205C). Bake bell peppers, turning occasionally, in pre-heated oven 10 to 15 minutes or until skin is charred and pepper is tender. Peel pepper and remove seeds. In a food processor fitted with a metal blade, process peppers to a puree. Or using a wooden spoon, press peppers through a sieve set over a bowl. In a small bowl, combine garlic, paprika, salt, pepper, dry mustard and olive oil. Beat in vinegar and pepper puree until mixture thickens slightly. Cover with plastic wrap and refrigerate until needed. Makes 1 cup.

Note: Serve with layered vegetable pâté or sliced avocado as a starter or use to toss green salad.

Twin Bean Dressing

Red Bean Dressing
1/3 cup red kidney beans, cooked
1 garlic clove, crushed
1/4 cup sunflower oil
1 tablespoon black currant vinegar
1/4 teaspoon salt
1/4 teaspoon black pepper

White Bean Dressing
1/3 cup white kidney beans, cooked
1/4 cup sunflower oil
2 tablespoons cottage cheese, sieved
1/4 teaspoon salt
1/4 teaspoon black pepper
1 teaspoon chopped fresh tansy
1 teaspoon chopped fresh carraway
1 teaspoon snipped fresh chives

In a food processor fitted with a metal blade, process red kidney beans, garlic and sunflower oil to a puree. Add vinegar, salt and pepper and process until smooth. Cover with plastic wrap and refrigerate until needed. Rinse food processor. Process white kidney beans and sunflower oil to a puree. Add cottage cheese, salt, pepper and herbs and process until smooth. Cover with plastic wrap and refrigerate until needed. Serve as separate dressings or partially blend together to give a marbled effect. Makes 2 cups.

Note: Serve with hot or cold vegetables, vegetarian nut burgers or nut and mushroom loaf. Use as a dip for all vegetables and salads.

Yellow Tarragon Dressing

2 (8-oz.) yellow bell peppers
1 teaspoon finely grated orange peel
1/2 cup almond oil
1 tablespoon tarragon vinegar
1/4 teaspoon salt
1/4 teaspoon black pepper
1 teaspoon Dijon-style mustard
1 tablespoon fresh chopped tarragon

Preheat oven to 400F (205C). Bake bell peppers, turning occasionally, in preheated oven 10 to 15 minutes or until skin is charred and peppers are tender. Peel peppers and remove seeds. In a food processor fitted with a metal blade, process peppers to a puree. Or, using a wooden spoon, press peppers through a sieve set over a bowl. In a small bowl, mix orange peel, almond oil, vinegar, salt, pepper and mustard with a wooden spoon until cloudy and slightly thick. Beat in pepper puree and tarragon until thick. Cover with plastic wrap and refrigerate until needed. Makes 1 cup.

Note: Serve with radicchio, chard, lettuce or grape leaves stuffed with lamb and rice filling.

Greek Dressing

4 cooked new potatoes
2 garlic cloves, crushed
1 tablespoon plus 1 teaspoon ground
   almonds
1/2 cup almond oil
Juice 1 orange
2 tablespoons white wine vinegar
2 tablespoons chopped fresh mint
Cold water, if needed

Mash potatoes in a small bowl. Beat in garlic, ground almonds and almond oil with a wooden spoon until smooth. Stir in orange juice, vinegar and mint until evenly blended. If needed, thin dressing with cold water. Cover with plastic wrap and refrigerate until needed. Makes 1-1/2 cups.

Note: Serve with fried or grilled fish, fried eggplant slices or globe artichokes. Also serve as a dip with a selection of raw vegetables.

Avocado & Bacon Dressing

4 slices crisp cooked bacon
1 teaspoon finely chopped green onion
1 teaspoon finely chopped seeded green chili pepper
1 tablespoon chopped fresh basil
1 teaspoon black pepper
1 medium-size avocado
1 teaspoon lemon juice
1 tablespoon green peppercorn vinegar

In a food processor fitted with a metal blade, process bacon until finely chopped. In a small bowl, combine chopped bacon, green onion, chili pepper, basil and pepper until thoroughly mixed. Peel avocado and remove seed. In food processor, process avocado, lemon juice and vinegar to a puree. Blend into bacon mixture. Serve immediately. Makes 1 cup.

Note: Serve with cooked asparagus spears, celery and green bean salad or shrimp salad.

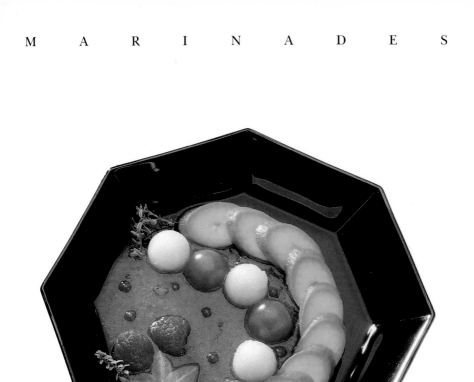

Star Fruit Dressing

1 star fruit, sliced
1/3 cup fresh raspberries
1/2 cup hazelnut oil
2 teaspoons pink peppercorns, crushed
1 tablespoon chopped fresh lemon thyme

In a food processor fitted with the metal blade, process star fruit and raspberries to a puree. Press fruit through a seive set over a small bowl with a wooden spoon. Whisk hazelnut oil and peppercorns into fruit juice until throughly blended. Cover with plastic wrap and refrigerate until needed. Just before using, stir in thyme. Makes 1 cup.

Note: Serve as a dressing for a fruit starter such as grapefruit and orange, melon, tomato and avocado or artichoke salad.

Mayonnaise

2 large egg yolks
1/2 teaspoon Dijon-style mustard
1/2 teaspoon salt
1/4 teaspoon black pepper
1/4 teaspoon cayenne pepper
1-1/4 cups olive oil
1 teaspoon fresh lemon juice
6 to 8 teaspoons white wine vinegar
Boiling water, if needed

By Hand: Have all ingredients at room temperature. In a medium-size bowl, blend egg yolks, mustard, salt and peppers with a wooden spoon. Add olive oil drop by drop, beating well after each addition of oil. Beat thoroughly until mixture begins to thicken, then, beating constantly, slowly increase flow of oil to a steady stream. When all oil has been added, beat in lemon juice and enough vinegar to desired flavor. If needed, thin with boiling water. Cover and refrigerate until needed. Makes 1-3/4 cups.

By Food Processor: In a food processor fitted with a metal blade, process egg yolks, mustard, salt and peppers until smooth. With processor running,

add olive oil drop by drop until mixture begins to thicken. Increase flow to a steady steam until all oil is added. Add lemon juice and enough vinegar to give desired flavor. If needed, thin dressing with boiling water. Cover with plastic wrap and refrigerate until needed. Makes 1-3/4 cups.

Variations: To prepare *Garlic Mayonnaise*, add 2 crushed garlic cloves to 2/3 cup mayonnaise.

To prepare *Lemon or Lime Mayonnaise*, add 2 teaspoons finely grated lemon or lime peel to 2/3 cup mayonnaise. Substitute lemon or lime juice for vinegar.

To prepare *Herbed Mayonnaise*, add 1 teaspoon chopped fresh tarragon, chervil, marjoram, parsley or chives to 2/3 cup mayonnaise.

To prepare *Green Mayonnaise*, add 1/4 cup mixed chopped watercress, basil, and parsley to 2/3 cup mayonnaise.

Quick Mayonnaise

2 large eggs
1/2 teaspoon dry mustard powder
1/2 teaspoon salt
1/2 teaspoon black pepper
1-1/4 cups olive oil
1 to 2 teaspoons white wine vinegar

Have all ingredients at room temperature. In a food processor fitted with a metal blade, process eggs, dry mustard, salt and pepper until smooth. With machine running, add olive oil drop by drop until mixture begins to thicken. Increase flow of oil to a steady steam until all oil has been added. Add enough vinegar to give desired flavor. Cover and refrigerate until needed. Makes 1-3/4 cups.

Variations: To prepare *Curried Mayonnaise*, add 1 teaspoon curry powder to 2/3 cup mayonnaise.

To prepare *Chili Pepper Mayonnaise*, add 1 teaspoon fresh chopped green chili pepper and 1 tablespoon chopped red pimento to 2/3 cup mayonnaise.

To prepare *Mustard Mayonnaise*, add 1 teaspoon dry mustard powder and 1 teaspoon Dijon-style mustard to 2/3 cup mayonnaise.

Basil & Tomato Mayonnaise

3 medium-size tomatoes
2 tablespoons plus 2 teaspoons fresh
 basil
1 garlic clove, crushed
1 tablespoon snipped fresh chives
1 teaspoon superfine sugar
2/3 cup Mayonnaise, page 46
2 tablespoons plain yogurt

In a large bowl, cover tomatoes with boiling water. Let stand 1 minute. Peel tomatoes, cut in half and remove seeds. Finely chop tomatoes and basil. In a medium-size bowl, combine tomatoes, basil, garlic, chives and sugar with a wooden spoon. Stir in mayonnaise and yogurt until all ingredients are evenly blended. Cover with plastic wrap and refrigerate until needed. Makes 1 cup.

Note: Use to coat pasta or rice salad or to toss cooked mixed vegetables. Serve as an accompaniment to lamb or chicken kebabs.

Celery Onion Mayonnaise

4 ozs. celery root, finely grated
2 teaspoons grated red onion
1 tablespoon chopped fresh mint
1/4 teaspoon cayenne pepper
2/3 cup Mayonnaise, page 46
2 tablespoons cottage cheese, sieved

In a medium-size bowl, combine celery root, onion, mint and cayenne pepper with a wooden spoon. Stir in mayonnaise and cottage cheese until all ingredients are well blended. Cover with plastic wrap and refrigerate until needed. Makes 1 cup.

Note: Serve with mixed bean salad, artichoke and mushroom salad, avocado and orange salad or asparagus spears.

Cocktail Dressing

1 teaspoon grated onion
1/4 teaspoon cayenne pepper
1/2 teaspoon anchovy paste
1/2 teaspoon hot-pepper sauce
2 tablespoons tomato paste
2 tablespoon olive oil
2 teaspoons white wine vinegar
2/3 cup Mayonnaise, page 46
2 teaspoons chopped fresh chervil
2 teaspoons chopped fresh parsley
2 teaspoons chopped fresh dill weed
1/4 cup whipping cream, whipped
    until stiff

In a small bowl, mix onion, cayenne pepper, anchovy paste, hot-pepper sauce, tomato paste, olive oil and vinegar until all ingredients are well blended. Stir in mayonnaise and chopped herbs until well blended. Fold whipped cream into mayonnaise mixture until smooth and evenly blended. Cover with plastic wrap and refrigerate until needed. Makes 1 cup.

Note: Use as an accompaniment to seafood salad.

Fennel & Orange Mayonnaise

6 cardamon pods
1 tablespoon plus 1 teaspoon finely
    chopped fennel bulb
1 tablespoon plus 1 teaspoon chopped
    fresh fennel leaves
1 teaspoon finely grated orange peel
2 tablespoons fresh orange juice
1 teaspoon superfine sugar
2/3 cup Mayonnaise, page 46
2 tablespoons cottage cheese, sieved

Split open cardamon pods. In a small bowl, crush seeds with a wooden spoon. Mix in chopped fennel bulb and leaves, orange peel and juice and sugar until well blended. Stir in mayonnaise and cottage cheese until evenly blended. Cover with plastic wrap and refrigerate until needed. Makes 1 cup.

Note: Serve with green salad, red and white cabbage and apple coleslaw or egg, meat, fish or pasta salad.

Italian Mayonnaise

1 pimento, chopped
1 tablespoon chopped dill pickle
1 tablespoon chopped pickled onions
2 teaspoons chopped Italian salami
2 teaspoons anchovy paste
2 teaspoons chopped anchovy fillets
1 tablespoon chopped fresh dill weed
8 stuffed green olives, chopped
2/3 cup Quick Mayonnaise, page 47

In a small bowl, combine pimento, dill pickle, pickled onions, salami, anchovy paste and fillets, dill weed and olives with a wooden spoon. Stir in mayonnaise until all ingredients are thoroughly blended. Cover with plastic wrap and refrigerate until needed. Makes 1 cup.

Note: Use for pasta or rice salad. Toss potatoes, mixed vegetables, peas and beans to coat evenly. Serve as an accompaniment with tuna, mackerel or chicken salad.

Bell Pepper Mayonnaise

1 (4-oz.) red bell pepper
1 teaspoon chili sauce
1/2 teaspoon hot-pepper sauce
1/2 teaspoon paprika
1 tablespoon plus 1 teaspoon chopped
   fresh oregano
2/3 cup Quick Mayonnaise, page 47

Preheat oven to 400F (205C). Bake bell pepper, turning occasionally, in preheated oven 10 to 15 minutes or until skin is charred and pepper is tender. Peel pepper, remove seeds and chop finely. Refrigerate until cold. In a small bowl, combine chopped pepper, chili sauce, hot-pepper sauce, paprika and oregano with a wooden spoon. Stir in mayonnaise until all ingredients are evenly blended. Cover with plastic wrap and refrigerate until needed. Makes 1 cup.

Variations: To prepare *Yellow Pepper Mayonnaise,* substitute 1 yellow bell pepper for red bell pepper.

To prepare *Green Pepper Mayonnaise,* substitute 1 green bell pepper for red bell pepper. Stir in 2 teaspoons peppercorns, crushed, and 1 teaspoon superfine sugar.

Note: Use with molded rice salad, mixed pasta salad and cooked mixed vegetable and potato salad.

Tartar Mayonnaise

2/3 cup Quick Mayonnaise, page 47
2 tablespoons capers
1 tablespoon plus 2 teaspoons gherkin
    pickles, chopped
2 teaspoons chopped fresh tarragon
2 teaspoons chopped fresh parsley
2 teaspoons chopped fresh chervil
2 teaspoons green peppercorns, crushed
2 tablespoons whipping cream, whipped
    until thick

In a small bowl, mix mayonnaise, capers, pickles, tarragon, parsley, chervil
and peppercorns with a wooden spoon
until all ingredients are well blended.
Gently fold whipped cream into mayonnaise mixture until smooth and
evenly blended. Cover with plastic
wrap and refrigerate until needed.
Makes 1 cup.

Variation: Substitute 3 tablespoons
plus 2 teaspoons sweet pickled vegetables or piccalilli for capers and gherkin pickles.

Note: Serve with all kinds of grilled or
fried fish or use as an accompaniment
to cold meat or fish salad.

Walnut Mayonnaise

2 tablespoons finely chopped walnuts
1 tablespoon chopped fresh rosemary
1 teaspoon honey
1 teaspoon finely grated orange peel
2/3 cup Mayonnaise, page 46, prepared
    with walnut oil instead of olive oil
2 tablespoons cottage cheese, sieved

In a small bowl, combine walnuts, rosemary, honey and orange peel with a wooden spoon. Stir in mayonnaise and cottage cheese until all ingredients are well blended. Cover with plastic wrap and refrigerate until needed. Makes 1 cup.

Variations: To prepare *Peanut Mayonnaise*, substitute peanut oil and finely chopped peanuts for walnut oil and walnuts.

To prepare *Hazelnut Mayonnaise*, substitute hazelnut oil and finely chopped hazelnuts for walnut oil and walnuts.

To prepare *Almond Mayonnaise*, substitute almond oil and finely chopped almonds for walnut oil and walnuts.

Note: Use to toss potato, bacon and sweet corn salad, hot or cold pasta, or as an accompaniment to cold chicken, turkey or duck.

Blue Cheese Dressing

1/2 teaspoon prepared mustard
1/2 teaspoon black pepper
1 teaspoon superfine sugar
2 tablespoons hazelnut oil
1 teaspoon tarragon vinegar
1/2 cup shredded Blue d'Auvergne
    cheese (2 ozs.)
1/3 cup whipping cream, whipped until
    thick

In a small bowl, beat mustard, pepper, sugar and hazelnut oil with a wooden spoon. Stir in vinegar and cheese until well blended. Fold whipped cream into cheese mixture until evenly blended. Cover with plastic wrap and refrigerate until needed. Makes about 2/3 cup.

Note: Serve with hard-cooked eggs or potato, fish, rice or pasta salad.

Garbanzo Bean Dip

1-1/4 cups cooked garbanzo beans
2 garlic cloves, crushed
1/2 teaspoon salt
1/2 teaspoon black pepper
1/2 cup sesame oil
2 tablespoons plus 2 teaspoons tahini
   paste
2 teaspoons orange juice
1/3 cup dairy sour cream

In a food processor fitted with a metal blade, process garbanzo beans to a puree. Or, using a wooden spoon, press beans through a sieve. Add garlic, salt and pepper and process. With motor running, add sesame oil drop by drop until all sesame oil has been incorporated. Or, using a wooden spoon, beat in sesame oil drop by drop. Stir in tahini paste, lemon juice and sour cream until evenly blended. Cover with plastic wrap and refrigerate until needed. Makes 1-1/4 cups.

Variation: To prepare as a dressing, add additional orange juice or cottage cheese to thin.

Note: Serve dip with cherry tomatoes, radishes, celery, bell peppers, zucchini or cucumber.

Curried Shrimp Dip

1 teaspoon tandoori paste
1 teaspoon grated onion
1 teaspoon grated gingerroot
1 teaspoon finely grated lemon peel
1 tablespoon fresh lemon juice
1/4 cup sunflower oil
2 (3-oz.) pkgs. Neufchâtel cheese,
    softened
1 tablespoon chopped fresh cilantro
2 teaspoons curry plant leaves
4 ozs. peeled cooked shrimp,
    coarsely chopped

In a medium-size bowl, mix tandoori paste, onion, gingerroot, lemon peel and juice with a wooden spoon. Beat in sunflower oil a little at a time until well blended. Add Neufchâtel cheese and beat until smooth. Stir in herbs and shrimp. Cover with plastic wrap and refrigerate until needed. Makes 1-1/4 cups.

Variations: To prepare a thin dressing, add enough plain yogurt to make desired consistency.

Substitute 4 coarsely chopped artichoke hearts for shrimp.

Note: Serve with fresh vegetables, cheese and chips.

Mushroom Dip

1/4 cup unsalted butter
6 ozs. button mushrooms, coarsely
  chopped
1/4 teaspoon hot-pepper sauce
1/4 teaspoon salt
1/2 teaspoon black pepper
2 teaspoons chopped green onions
1 teaspoon finely grated lime peel
2 teaspoons fresh lime juice
1 (3-oz.) pkg. cream cheese, softened
1 tablespoon plus 1 teaspoon chopped
  fresh chervil
Fresh chervil sprigs and lime slices to
  garnish

Melt butter in a small saucepan. Saute mushrooms in butter 1 minute. In a food processor fitted with metal blades, process mushrooms, hot-pepper sauce, salt, pepper and green onions to a puree. Add lime peel and juice, cream cheese and chervil and process until well blended and smooth. Garnish with chervil sprigs and lime slices. Makes 1-1/4 cups.

Note: Serve dip with toast, crackers or radishes, cauliflower floweretes, zucchini sticks, celery and tomatoes. Also serve as a thick dressing to accompany green salad.

Taramosalata

4 ozs. smoked cod roe
1/4 cup dry bread crumbs
2 tablespoons plus 2 teaspoons cold water
2 teaspoons fresh lemon juice
1 garlic clove, crushed
1/2 teaspoon black pepper
1/3 cup olive oil
1 (3-oz.) pkg. Neufchâtel cheese, softened
6 black olives and fresh parsley sprigs to garnish

Using a sharp knife, cut through cod roe skin. Scrape out all roe into a food processor fitted with a metal blade. In a small bowl, mix bread crumbs and water. Add moistened bread crumbs, lemon juice, garlic and pepper to roe. Process several seconds or until mixture is well blended. Or, using a wooden spoon, press roe through a sieve into a small bowl and beat in remaining ingredients. With machine running, add olive oil drop by drop until all olive oil has been incorporated. Or, using a wooden spoon, add olive oil drop by drop, beating well. Beat in Neufchâtel cheese until mixture is smooth and creamy. Spoon into a dish, cover with plastic wrap and refrigerate until needed. Garnish with black olives and parsley sprigs. Makes 1-1/4 cups.

Variation: To serve as a thin dressing, add enough plain yogurt to make desired consistency and serve with avocados or asparagus spears.

Note: Serve with toast, crackers or sticks of fresh vegetables.

Egg & Mustard Dressing

2 hard-cooked egg yolks
1 raw egg yolk
2 teaspoons dry mustard
2 tablespoons olive oil
1 teaspoon Worcestershire sauce
1 teaspoon white wine vinegar
2 green onions, finely chopped
2/3 cup whipping cream, whipped until
   thick

In a small bowl, beat hard-cooked and raw egg yolks and mustard with a wooden spoon. Beat in olive oil drop by drop until all olive oil is incorporated and mixture is smooth and creamy. Stir in Worcestershire sauce, vinegar and green onions. Gently fold whipped cream into egg mixture until mixture is well blended. Makes 1 cup.

Variation: To prepare *Lemon Mustard Dressing,* substitute 1 teaspoon lemon juice for vinegar. Add 1 teaspoon finely grated lemon peel, 1 teaspoon honey and 1 tablespoon chopped fresh herbs.

Note: Serve as an accompaniment to cold beef, pork or chicken salad or use as a substitute for egg mayonnaise.

Pink Cream Dressing

2 tablespoons grated fresh beet
2 tablespoons grated Red Delicious apple
2 teaspoons grated onion
1 garlic clove, crushed
1/2 teaspoon grated mace
1/2 teaspoon black pepper
1/4 teaspoon salt
1 teaspoon superfine sugar
2/3 cup whipping cream, whipped until
   thick

In a small bowl, mix beet, apple, onion, garlic, mace, pepper, salt and sugar using a wooden spoon. Carefully fold whipped cream into beet mixture until evenly blended. Stir before using. Makes 1/3 cup.

Note: Serve as an alternative to mayonnaise. This dressing goes especially well with fish salad, tuna and mackerel.

Smoked Seafood Dressing

4 ozs. smoked trout
2 teaspoons finely grated lime peel
2 tablespoons fresh lime juice
2/3 cup half and half
1 tablespoon snipped fresh chives
2 tablespoons chopped fresh watercress
1/4 teaspoon cayenne pepper
Fresh watercress sprigs and lime wedges
    to garnish

In a food processor fitted with a metal blade, process trout and lime peel and juice to a smooth puree. Add half and half and process until well blended. Stir in chives, watercress and cayenne pepper. Garnish with watercress and lime wedges. Makes 1 cup.

Variation: Substitute smoked salmon or mackerel for trout.

Note: Serve with any seafood salad or with grilled fish. This dressing also makes a good accompaniment to a mixed vegetable and bean or green salad.

MARINADES

Marinades are capable of changing the appearance, flavor and texture of all types of ingredients. They can also act as a seal, preventing moisture escaping from the food during cooking.

The marinades in this book fall into three main categories—liquid marinades, dry marinades and pastes and glazes.

Liquid Marinades

Based on a mixture of oils, wine vinegar, herbs and seasonings or fruit juices and grated peel, these are ideal for marinating meat, fish, poultry, game and vegetables to impart flavor and add moisture. The marinade protects the food while it is being cooked over a barbecue, grill or in the oven.

Dry Marinades and Pastes

These are simply a blend of mixed dried herbs or spices in the form of leaves, berries, seed and pods. When crushed in a pestle and mortar, this mixture produces an intense blend of dry ingredients, and with the addition of salt, pepper or sugar, determines the sharpness or sweetness of the mixture required. Rubbed into the surface of meat or fish, or used to toss vegetables to coat evenly, these mixtures impart an instant flavor which penetrates the food during marinating and cooking.

To make a paste marinade, mix the above blend of ingredients with fruit peel and juice and garlic or oil to moisten the mixture enough to form a paste. Spread on the surface of meat, fish or poultry to coat evenly.

Glazes

Quick and easy to prepare, these are brushed on to the food's surface before and during cooking. They form a rich glaze, crisp texture and intensely flavored surface on all

foods being cooked. Use thick and clear honey, jellies and preserves, fruit juices and peels and chopped fresh herbs or crushed spices.

Herbs

These should be fairly intense in flavor such as fresh or dried bay leaves, rosemary, tarragon, oregano basil, thyme, sage or marjoram. Use stems of rosemary to thread onto kebabs—they give the food wonderful aromatic flavor. Any mixture of chopped fresh herbs are invaluable to most marinades.

Oils

These add moisture and give protection to marinated foods, especially during cooking when they lubricate the food and prevent it from drying out. Any oil may be used, again the flavor and quality depend on the choice of oil.

Vinegars and Fruit Juices

These acid ingredients act as tenderizing agents for food. They impart flavor and mix well with oils. Grated peel from the fruits adds texture and extra flavor, and any leftover marinade may be used as a sauce.

Spices

Dried spices in the form of seeds, berries, pods, leaves or bark can be crushed to give a dry mixture. Natural choices are whole cloves, nutmeg, mace, cinnamon sticks, allspice and juniper berries, coriander, mustard and cumin seeds, just to name a few. Dried spices have an intense flavor which they impart to all foods being marinated.

Other useful flavorsome ingredients are fresh gingerroot, garlic, chilies, bell peppers, creamed or grated coconut and curry paste. These mix well with meat, fish, vegetables and poultry.

Apple & Elderflower Pork

1 pork loin, boned
1 tablespoons plus 1 teaspoon
   all-purpose flour
2/3 cup water
Elderflowers and apple slices tossed in
   lemon juice to garnish

Marinade:
1-1/4 cups elderflower wine
2 heads elderflowers
1 tablespoon plus 1 teaspoon honey
2 tablespoons almond oil
3 fresh bay leaves

Stuffing:
2 cups chopped cooking apple
2 tablespoons elderflower wine
1 teaspoon honey
1 tablespoon chopped fresh chives
1/2 cup fresh bread crumbs

Trim any excess fat from pork, leaving a thin layer of fat on outside. Score with a knife to make a lattice pattern. To prepare marinade, in a large bowl, combine wine, elderflowers, honey, almond oil and bay leaves. Immerse pork in marinade, cover and refrigerate 4 hours or overnight. Preheat oven to 375F (190C). To prepare stuffing, in a small saucepan, bring apples, wine and honey to a boil. Cook, stirring occasionally, until apple is pulpy and soft and all liquid has been absorbed. Stir in chives and bread crumbs until well blended. Cool. Remove meat from marinade. Pat dry with paper towels. Spread stuffing over center of meat. Roll up and tie securely with thin string in several places. Place in a roasting pan and brush well with marinade. Bake in preheated oven 1 hour, basting with more marinade if necessary. Remove meat from pan. To prepare sauce, stir flour into juices. Add remaining marinade and water. Bring to a boil, stirring constantly. Cook 2 minutes and strain. Cut meat in thin slices. Garnish with elderflowers and apple slices. Serve with sauce. Makes 6 servings.

Variation: If elderflowers are out of season, substitute 2 tablespoons plus 2 teaspoons elderberries or use dried elderflowers.

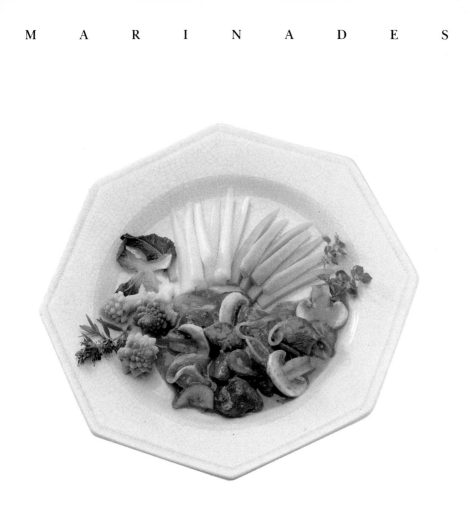

Beef in Wine

1-1/2 lbs. cubed beef stew meat
1 tablespoon butter
6 ozs. button mushrooms
2/3 cup beef stock
2 tablespoons all-purpose flour
1 tablespoon tomato paste
Fresh oregano and winter savory sprigs
   to garnish

Marinade:
2/3 cup red wine
1/2 medium-size cucumber, thinly sliced
1 medium-size red onion, thinly sliced
1 tablespoon chopped fresh oregano
1 tablespoon chopped fresh winter
   savory
1 garlic clove
2 teaspoons light-brown sugar
1/2 teaspoon salt
1/2 teaspoon black pepper

To prepare marinade, in a large casserole dish, combine all marinade ingredients. Stir in meat. Cover and refrigerate 4 hours. Preheat oven to 350F (175C). Strain marinade into a bowl. Melt butter in a large saucepan. Add meat, onion and herbs from marinade and mushrooms. Fry quickly to brown meat. Add marinade and beef stock. Bring to a boil and return mixture to casserole dish. Cover and bake in preheated oven 2 hours or until meat is tender. In a 1-cup measure, blend flour and tomato paste. Stir into beef mixture to thicken gravy. Garnish with oregano and winter savory sprigs and serve hot. Makes 4 to 6 servings.

Horseradish Steak

1 lb. round steak, cut in thin strips
1 tablespoon butter
2 tablespoons sherry
Fresh thyme sprigs to garnish

Marinade:
1 tablespoon plus 1 teaspoon horseradish
1 tablespoon plus 1 teaspoon plain
   yogurt
2 teaspoons paprika
1 tablespoon chopped fresh thyme
1/2 teaspoon salt
1/2 teaspoon black pepper

To prepare marinade, in a small bowl, combine all marinade ingredients until well blended. Add meat and stir to coat evenly. Cover and refrigerate 1 hour or until ready to cook. Melt butter in a large skillet. Remove meat from marinade and cook quickly 1 minute. Transfer meat to a serving dish. Stir remaining marinade and sherry into pan juices. Bring to a boil, stirring constantly. Pour sauce over meat. Garnish with thyme sprigs. Makes 4 servings.

Juniper Lamb

1 (1-1/4-lb.) loin of lamb, boned, trimmed
1 tablespoon plus 1 teaspoon all-purpose
   flour
1/4 cup water
Lemon wedges, apricots and fresh
   rosemary sprigs to garnish

Marinade:
1 cup rosé wine
1 tablespoon plus 1 teaspoon juniper
   berries, crushed
2 teaspoons angostura bitters
2 bay leaves
1/2 teaspoon salt
1/2 teaspoon black pepper

Stuffing:
1/2 cup fresh bread crumbs
2 ozs. dried apricots, presoaked
2 teaspoons lemon juice
2 teaspoons finely grated lemon peel
2 teaspoons chopped fresh rosemary

To prepare marinade, in a large bowl, combine all marinade ingredients until well blended. Immerse lamb in marinade, turning to coat evenly. Cover and refrigerate 4 hours or overnight. Preheat oven to 375F (190C). To prepare stuffing, in a food processor fitted with a metal blade, process all stuffing ingredients until well blended. Remove lamb from marinade. Pat dry with paper towels. Spread stuffing over center of meat. Roll up and tie securely with cotton string in several places. Place in a roasting pan. Brush well with marinade. Bake in preheated oven 45 to 50 minutes, basting with more marinade if necessary. Remove lamb from pan and keep warm. Add remaining marinade to pan juices. Bring to a boil, stirring constantly. Dissolve flour in water and stir into sauce. Strain sauce into a warmed serving bowl. Remove string from meat and cut in thin slices. Garnish with lemon wedges, apricots and rosemary sprigs and serve with sauce. Makes 4 to 6 servings.

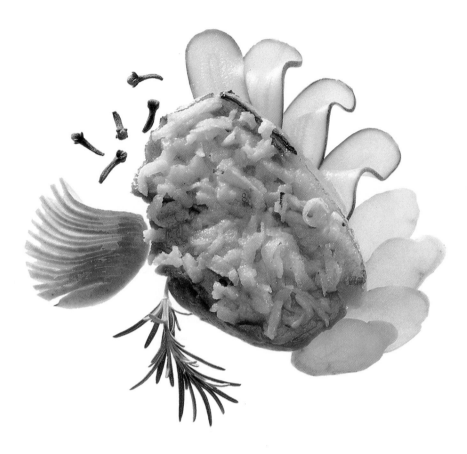

Marinated Ham Steaks

4 (5-oz.) ham steaks
Fresh rosemary sprigs to garnish

Marinade:
2 teaspoons light soy sauce
1 tablespoon sherry vinegar
2 tablespoons peanut oil
1 tablespoon honey
1 tablespoon chopped fresh rosemary
6 whole cloves
1 (1-inch) piece cinnamon stick
1/2 teaspoon black pepper
1 (8-oz.) cooking apple, peeled, grated

Soak ham steaks in cold water for several hours or overnight. Drain and dry on paper towels. Place in a shallow dish. To prepare marinade, in a medium-size bowl, combine all marinade ingredients until well blended. Pour marinade over ham steaks in dish, turning to coat evenly. Cover and refrigerate 1 hour. Preheat a barbecue. Cook ham steaks 3 to 5 minutes, turning once and brushing with extra marinade. Garnish with rosemary sprigs. Makes 4 servings.

Peppercorn Steaks

4 (4-oz.) beef tenderloin steaks
1 tablespoon butter
1 tablespoon whipping cream
Pink and green peppercorns to garnish

Marinade:
1 tablespoon whole-grain mustard
2 teaspoons green peppercorns, crushed
2 teaspoons pink peppercorns, crushed
1 tablespoon tomato paste
1/2 teaspoon salt
2 teaspoons chopped fresh marjoram
2 teaspoons chopped fresh oregano
2 teaspoons chopped fresh basil

To prepare marinade, in a small bowl, combine all marinade ingredients until well mixed. Spread marinade evenly over each steak to coat. Melt butter in large skillet. Cook steaks quickly to seal surfaces. Turn steaks over and cook 3 to 5 minutes or to desired doneness. Remove steaks and keep warm. Stir whipping cream into pan juices and bring to a boil. Spoon sauce over steaks. Garnish with peppercorns. Makes 4 servings.

Peppered Pork

4 (4-oz.) pork sirloin cutlets
Orange slices and fresh ginger mint
   sprigs to garnish

Marinade:
1 small yellow bell pepper
1 small red bell pepper
1 garlic clove
1 tablespoon plus 1 teaspoon olive oil
2 teaspoons grated orange peel
2 tablespoons fresh orange juice
2 teaspoons honey
2 tablespoons chopped fresh ginger mint

Preheat oven to 400F (205C). In a medium-size baking dish, bake bell peppers in preheated oven 10 to 15 minutes or until skin is charred and peels off easily. Cool slightly. Peel bell peppers and remove stalk and seeds. In a food processor fitted with a metal blade, process bell peppers until smooth. Add garlic, olive oil, orange peel and juice, honey and ginger mint. Process to a puree. Place pork in a medium-size baking dish. Pour bell pepper puree over pork, turning pork to coat evenly. Cover and refrigerate 30 minutes. In a large skillet, cook pork 15 minutes or until tender, turning over once. Garnish with orange slices and ginger mint sprigs. Makes 4 servings.

Lime & Pomegranate Lamb

4 (5-oz.) double loin lamb chops
2 tablespoons butter
1 small red onion, thinly sliced
2 tablespoons all-purpose flour
Red currant strands, pomegranate seeds
    and fresh herb sprigs to garnish

Marinade:
2 pomegranates, peeled
Finely grated peel 1 lime
1 tablespoon fresh lime juice
1 tablespoon red currant jelly
1 tablespoon chopped fresh thyme
1/2 teaspoon black pepper
1/4 teaspoon salt

To prepare marinade, scrape pomegranate seeds into a sieve set over a bowl. Reserve a few seeds for garnish. Using a wooden spoon, press pomegranate through sieve to extract all juice. Measure 1 tablespoon plus 1 teaspoon of juice into a small bowl. Reserve remaining pomegrantate juice. Stir in lime peel and juice, jelly, thyme, pepper and salt. Mix well. Place chops in a shallow dish. Brush each chop with marinade to coat evenly. Cover and refrigerate 1 hour. Preheat a barbecue to moderately hot. Cook chops 5 to 8 minutes on each side, brushing with remaining marinade. Keep warm. Melt butter in a small saucepan. Saute onion 1 to 2 minutes or until tender. Stir in flour. Cook 1 minute and remove from heat. Add enough water to reserved pomegranate juice to measure 1 cup. Stir into onion mixture. Bring to a boil, stirring constantly, and cook 2 minutes. Garnish with red currant strands, reserved pomegranate seeds and fresh herb sprigs and serve with sauce. Makes 4 servings.

Pork Tenderloin with Herbs

1 (1-lb.) pork tenderloin, trimmed
1 tablespoon plus 1 teaspoon all-purpose
  flour
Water, if needed
1 teaspoon half and half

Marinade:
2 tablespoons olive oil
1 tablespoon Madeira wine
1/2 teaspoon salt
1/2 teaspoon black pepper
1 teaspoon Dijon-style mustard
1 teaspoon superfine sugar
1 tablespoon grated onion
1 tablespoon chopped fresh sage
1 tablespoon chopped fresh oregano

Place pork in a shallow baking dish. To prepare marinade, in a small bowl, combine all marinade ingredients until well blended. Pour over pork tenderloin, turning to coat well. Cover and refrigerate 2 to 3 hours. Preheat oven to 425F (220C). Bake pork in preheated oven 15 minutes, basting with marinade if necessary. Remove pork and keep warm. Stir flour into marinade in dish. Pour into a saucepan. Bring to a boil and cook 2 minutes, stirring constantly. If sauce is too thick, add a small amount of water. Remove pan from heat and stir in half and half. Slice pork in 1/2-inch thick slices. Serve with sauce. Makes 4 servings.

Rosy Roasted Ham Steak

1 (2-1/2 to 3-lb.) ham steak
Whole cloves
2 teaspoons arrowroot
2/3 cup water
2 tablespoons red currant jelly
Fresh oregano sprigs to garnish

Marinade:
2 cups red currants
2 tablespoons light-brown sugar
3 tablespoon chopped fresh oregano
1 tablespoon olive oil

Soak ham in cold water several hours or overnight. Drain and rinse in fresh water. Place in a large saucepan, cover with cold water and bring to a boil. Cover and simmer 30 minutes. Remove ham from water, cool and remove rind. To prepare marinade, press red currants through a sieve set over a bowl. Stir brown sugar, oregano and olive oil into red currant juice. Add ham and turn in marinade to coat. Cover and refrigerate 1 hour. Preheat oven to 375F (190C). Using a sharp knife, score fat on ham in a lattice pattern. Press cloves evenly into each diamond shape and brush with marinade. In a roasting pan, bake ham in preheated oven 45 to 50 minutes, brushing with extra marinade if required. Cover with foil if surface becomes too brown. Remove ham and keep warm. In a 1-cup glass measure, blend arrowroot and water. Add to pan juices with marinade, stirring to mix well. Strain into a saucepan. Stir in jelly. Bring to a boil, stirring constantly, and cook 1 minute. Pour sauce around ham and garnish with oregano sprigs. Makes 8 servings.

Saffron Lamb Cutlets

8 (2-1/2 oz.) leg sirloin lamb chops
8 sheets fillo pastry
1/4 cup butter, melted
Fresh rosemary sprigs and orange slices
   to garnish

Marinade:
2/3 cup dairy sour cream
2 teaspoons finely grated orange peel
1 tablespoon fresh orange juice
1/2 teaspoon saffron thread or a good
   pinch of powdered saffron
2 teaspoons chopped fresh rosemary
1/4 teaspoon salt
1/4 teaspoon black pepper

Trim excess fat from each chop. Strip off fat and skin from bone above eye of meat, leaving bones completely clean. To prepare marinade, in a small bowl, combine all marinade ingredients until evenly blended. Place chops in a large shallow dish. Spread marinade over both sides of chops. Cover and refrigerate 3 to 4 hours. Preheat oven to 450F (230C). Cover a baking sheet with foil. Arrange chops apart and bake in preheated oven on top shelf 5 to 8 minutes or until marinade is set and chop is tinged with brown. Cool 15 minutes. Brush each piece of fillo pastry with butter and fold in half. Wrap each chop in pastry, leaving bone uncovered. Butter baking sheet. Arrange pastry wrapped chops on buttered baking sheet. Brush with remaining butter and return to oven 10 to 12 minutes or until pastry is crisp and golden brown. Garnish with rosemary sprigs and orange slices. Makes 8 servings.

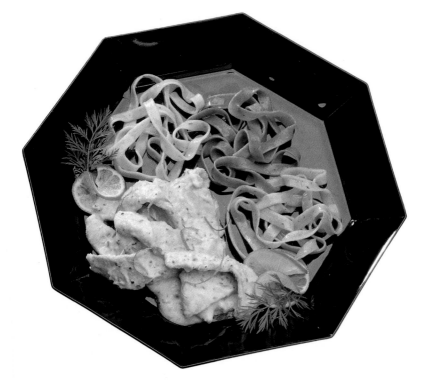

Spiced Ham Steak

1 (1-1/4-lb.) ham steak
3 ozs. creamed coconut
2 tablespoons mango chutney
Juice 1 lime
3 tablespoons dairy sour cream
Lime slices and fresh herb sprigs to
    garnish

Marinade:
2 teaspoons cumin seeds, toasted
1 teaspoon ground allspice
1/2 teaspoon mustard seeds
1/2 teaspoon white peppercorns
1/2 teaspoons black peppercorns
2 teaspoons grated lime peel
2 tablespoons butter, melted

Soak ham in cold water several hours or overnight. Drain and rinse in fresh water. Place in large saucepan. Cover with water and bring to a boil. Cover and simmer 30 minutes. Remove ham from water. Cool, then cut in thin strips. In a pestle and mortar, combine cumin, allspice, mustard seeds and peppercorns. Crush finely and work in lime peel and butter until well blended and smooth. Rub marinade into ham strips and place in a medium-size bowl. Cover and refrigerate 2 to 3 hours. Heat a nonstick skillet. Fry ham strips quickly 2 to 3 minutes. Stir in coconut, chutney and lime juice. Bring to a boil and cook 2 to 3 minutes. Remove from heat and stir in sour cream. Garnish with lime slices and herb sprigs and serve with sauce. Makes 4 servings.

Spiced Skewered Lamb

2 (1/2-lb.) lamb shoulder neck fillets
Fresh mint leaves, apple wedges tossed
   in lemon juice and lemon wedges to
   garnish

Marinade:
1 teaspoon ground allspice
1 teaspoon grated gingerroot
1 tablespoon honey
2 tablespoons sherry vinegar
1/3 cup apple juice
1 tablespoon plus 1 teaspoon olive oil
2 tablespoons chopped fresh mint

Trim excess fat from lamb. Cut in very thin strips about 3 inches long. To prepare marinade, in a medium-size bowl, combine all marinade ingredients until evenly blended. Turn lamb strips in marinade to coat each piece evenly. Cover and refrigerate 2 to 3 hours. Meanwhile, soak 8 wooden skewers in cold water. Prepare a barbecue. Thread several pieces of lamb onto each skewer. Cook lamb 2 to 3 minutes, turning once and brushing with more marinade if necessary. Pour remaining marinade into a small saucepan. Bring to a boil. Garnish lamb with mint leaves and apple and lemon wedges and serve with marinade. Makes 4 servings.

Sweet & Sour Spare Ribs

1-1/2 lbs. pork spare ribs
Green onion flowers to garnish

Marinade:
1 tablespoon soy sauce
2 teaspoons honey
1 tablespoon dry sherry
3 tablespoons tomato paste
1 garlic clove, crushed
1 small green chili pepper, seeded,
    chopped
2 teaspoons grated gingerroot
1 (1-inch) piece cinnamon stick
6 cloves
1/2 teaspoon mustard seeds
1/2 teaspoon salt
1 teaspoon black peppercorns

Trim ribs and place in a shallow dish. To prepare marinade, in a small bowl, combine soy sauce, honey, sherry, tomato paste, garlic, chili pepper and gingerroot. In a pestle and mortar, crush cinnamon, cloves, mustard seeds, salt and peppercorns until ground and well blended. Stir spices into marinade until evenly blended. Pour marinade over ribs, turning ribs to coat evenly. Cover and refrigerate 2 to 3 hours. Prepare a barbecue. Cook ribs 5 to 8 minutes, turning once and brushing with more marinade if necessary, until crisp. Garnish with green onion flowers. Makes 4 servings.

Chicken Bites

1-1/2 lbs. boneless chicken breasts,
   Cut in thin strips
24 kumquats
Cooked pasta, if desired
Sliced kumquats and fresh herb sprigs to
   garnish

Marinade:
2/3 cup plain yogurt, strained
2 teaspoons tomato paste
2 teaspoons Worcestershire sauce
2 tablespoons mango chutney
1/2 teaspoon salt
1/2 teaspoon black pepper
1 tablespoon plus 1 teaspoon chopped
   fresh oregano
1 tablespoon plus 1 teaspoon chopped
   fresh winter savory

Soak 12 wooden skewers in water. To prepare marinade, in a medium bowl, combine all marinade ingredients until well blended. Stir in chicken until evenly coated. Refrigerate 3 hours. Prepare a barbecue. Thread a kumquat and 2 or 3 chicken strips onto each skewer. Place remaining kumquats on end of each skewer. Cook skewers, turning once, 5 to 8 minutes or until chicken is done. Brush with marinade during cooking, if necessary. Serve hot with cooked pasta, if desired. Garnish with sliced kumquats and herb sprigs. Makes 4 servings.

—— Crispy Grapefruit Chicken ——

8 chicken thighs
Grapefruit segments and fresh rosemary
   sprigs to garnish

Marinade:
1 tablespoon chopped fresh rosemary
1 tablespoon honey
1/4 cup olive oil
3/4 teaspoon cayenne pepper
2 teaspoons finely grated grapefruit peel
2 tablespoons grapefruit juice

To prepare marinade, in a small bowl, combine all marinade ingredients until well blended. Arrange chicken in a shallow baking dish. Cover chicken with marinade and turn chicken until evenly coated. Cover and refrigerate 3 to 4 hours. Preheat oven to 425F (220C) or prepare a barbecue. Cook chicken 20 to 25 minutes or until golden brown and skin is crisp, basting with more marinade if necessary. Garnish with grapefruit segments and rosemary sprigs. Makes 4 servings.

Curried Chicken Drumsticks

8 chicken drumsticks
1/4 cup butter, softened
1 garlic clove, crushed
1 tablespoon chopped fresh cilantro
1/3 cup fresh bread crumbs
Fresh flat-leaf parsley sprigs and lime
    wedges to garnish

Marinade:
1 teaspoon mild curry paste
2 teaspoons finely grated lime peel
1 tablespoon fresh lime juice
1 tablespoon plus 1 teaspoon creamed
    coconut
1 teaspoon honey
1/2 teaspoon salt
1/2 teaspoon black pepper

Wipe chicken drumsticks with paper towels to dry. To prepare marinade, in a small bowl, combine all marinade ingredients with a wooden spoon to form a paste. Spread marinade evenly over each drumstick to coat. Cover and refrigerate 3 to 4 hours. Preheat oven to 400F (205C). In a small bowl, blend butter, garlic and cilantro until soft and smooth. Spoon into a baking dish and melt in preheated oven. Coat each drumstick evenly with bread crumbs. Roll in butter mixture. Bake 30 minutes or until golden brown and tender. Garnish with flat-leaf parsley sprigs and lime wedges. Makes 8 servings.

Devilled Turkey Breast

1-1/2 lbs. sliced turkey breast
1/3 cup butter, melted
1/4 cup tomato sauce
2 tablespoons Worcestershire sauce
1 tablespoon soy sauce
2 tablespoons mango chutney
Fresh watercress sprigs to garnish

Marinade:
2 teaspoons ground ginger
2 teaspoons white pepper
2 teaspoons dry mustard powder
1 teaspoon salt
1 teaspoon curry powder
1 tablespoon light-brown sugar

To prepare marinade, in a plastic bag, combine all marinade ingredients. Shake until well mixed. Shake 1 turkey slice in bag at a time, shaking well to coat evenly with marinade. Cover and refrigerate 1 hour. Preheat broiler. Brush each turkey slice generously with butter. Broil on a broiler pan, turning frequently, 10 to 12 minutes or until golden brown and tender. Remove from pan and keep warm. Stir tomato sauce, Worcestershire, soy sauce and chutney into pan juices. Cook under broiler until sauce bubbles, then pour over turkey slices. Garnish with watercress sprigs. Makes 4 servings.

Duck with Cranberries & Orange

1 (2-lb.) duck, cut in quarters
2 teaspoons arrowroot
2 teaspoons fresh orange juice
Orange slices, fresh cranberries and
    fresh sage leaves to garnish

Marinade:
1 cup fresh cranberries
2/3 cup water
2 tablespoons plus 2 teaspoons honey
2 teaspoons finely grated orange peel
2 tablespoons fresh orange juice
2/3 cup rosé wine
1 tablespoon plus 1 teaspoon chopped
    fresh sage leaves
1/2 teaspoon salt
1/2 teaspoon black pepper

Trim excess fat and skin from duck. To prepare marinade, in a small saucepan, bring cranberries, water and honey to a boil. Simmer about 10 minutes or until cranberries are tender. Using a wooden spoon, press cranberries through a sieve set over a bowl. Stir in orange peel and juice, wine, sage, salt and pepper. Add duck to marinade, turning duck to coat evenly. Cover and refrigerate 4 hours or overnight. Preheat oven to 425F (220C). Arrange duck in a large baking dish. Bake in preheated oven 45 minutes. Pour remaining marinade over duck. Cover and return to oven. Reduce temperature to 375F (190C). Bake 40 minutes or until duck is tender. Remove duck and keep warm. Blend arrowroot and orange juice in a small saucepan. Pour off most of fat from marinade into a dish. Stir marinade into orange juice. Bring to a boil, stirring constantly, and simmer 1 minute. Pour sauce over duck and garnish with orange slices, cranberries and sage leaves. Makes 4 servings.

Golden Turkey

4 (4-oz.) boneless turkey steaks
1 garlic clove, minced
1/4 cup butter, softened
1/3 cup potato chips, crushed
Fresh flat-leaf parsley and watercress
    sprigs and lime wedges to garnish

Marinade:
12 cardamon pods
2 teaspoons coriander seeds
1/2 teaspoon mustard seeds
1 garlic clove, crushed
1 tablespoon grated lime peel
1/2 teaspoon salt
1/2 teaspoon black pepper

To prepare marinade, remove seeds from cardamon pods. Crush in a pestle and mortar with coriander and mustard seeds until finely blended. Blend in garlic, lime peel, salt and pepper. Cut a slit in each steak to form a pocket. Spread marinade mixture over steaks, rubbing into flesh. Cover and refrigerate 2 to 3 hours. Preheat oven to 425F (220C). In a small bowl, blend garlic and butter. Spread steak evenly with 1/2 of garlic butter, then fill cavities with remainder. Coat steaks evenly in crushed potato chips and arrange in a medium roasting pan, cavity side up. Bake in preheated oven 15 minutes or until golden brown and crisp. Garnish with parsley and watercress sprigs and lime wedges. Makes 4 servings.

Turkey Stroganoff

3 (1/2-lb.) turkey fillets
2 tablespoons butter
1 tablespoon olive oil
6 ozs. button mushrooms
1 tablespoon fresh lemon juice
2/3 cup pineapple juice
2/3 cup chicken stock
2/3 cup half and half
1 egg yolk
Flesh from 1/2 pineapple, chopped
1/2 cup flaked toasted almonds and fresh
    parsley sprigs to garnish

Marinade:
2 tablespoons all-purpose flour
1/2 teaspoon ground cloves
1 teaspoon ground nutmeg
1/2 teaspoon salt
1/2 teaspoon black pepper
2 teaspoons grated lemon peel

Cut turkey in very thin slices. To prepare marinade, in a medium bowl, combine all marinade ingredients until well blended. Add turkey, turning turkey to coat evenly. Refrigerate 1 hour. Heat butter and olive oil in a large skillet. Cook turkey and mushrooms quickly, stirring occasionally. Stir in lemon and pineapple juices and chicken stock. Bring to a boil, cover and simmer 5 minutes. In a small bowl, beat half and half and egg yolk. Stir into turkey mixture and remove from heat. Stir 1/2 of chopped pineapple. Garnish with remaining chopped pineapple, almonds and parsley sprigs. Makes 6 servings.

Pheasant in Madeira with Figs & Cherries

1 oven-ready pheasant
1 tablespoon butter
1 fresh fig, sliced, fresh sweet cherries,
   grapefruit segments and watercress
   sprigs to garnish

Marinade:
1 teaspoon honey
2 teaspoons finely grated grapefruit peel
2 tablespoons chopped fresh purple basil
   leaves
2 tablespoons snipped fresh chives
1 teaspoon dry mustard powder
1/2 teaspoon salt
1/2 teaspoon black pepper
2/3 cup Madeira wine
2 tablespoons olive oil
4 figs, cut in quarters
1 cup fresh sweet cherries, pitted
1 tablespoon plus 1 teaspoon all-purpose
   flour
2 tablespoons half and half

Cut pheasant in 4 pieces. Trim excess skin and remove wing tips. To prepare marinade, in a medium-size bowl, combine honey, grapefruit peel, basil, chives, dry mustard, salt, pepper, wine and olive oil until well blended. Stir in figs and cherries. Immerse pheasant in marinade, turning pheasant to coat evenly. Cover and refrigerate 4 hours. Preheat oven to 350F (175C). Melt butter in a large skillet. Fry pheasant quickly to brown evenly. Add marinade, bring to a boil and pour into a large casserole dish. Bake in preheated oven 1 hour or until pheasant is tender. Remove pheasant and keep warm. Spoon fat from marinade. In a small bowl, blend flour and half and half. Add to marinade mixture. Bring to a boil, stirring constantly. Cook until sauce thickens, then simmer 2 minutes. Pour sauce over pheasant and garnish with fig, cherries, grapefruit segments and watercress sprigs. Makes 4 servings.

Chicken Provencal

1 (3-lb.) broiler-fryer chicken
1 red bell pepper
4 tomatoes, peeled, seeded, sliced
Fresh basil leaves to garnish

Marinade:
10 pitted black olives, cut in half
5 anchovy fillets, chopped
3 tablespoons olive oil
3 tablespoons sweet sherry
1 garlic clove, crushed
1/2 teaspoon black pepper
2 tablespoons chopped fresh basil

Cut chicken in half. To prepare marinade, in a medium-size bowl, mix all marinade ingredients until well mixed. Add chicken, turning chicken in marinade to coat evenly. Cover and refrigerate 4 hours. Preheat oven to 425F (220C). Place bell pepper on a baking sheet. Bake in preheated oven until skin is charred and bell pepper is tender. Cool. Arrange chicken in a large baking dish. Spoon a small amount of marinade over chicken. Bake in preheated oven 30 to 40 minutes or until golden brown, crisp and tender. Keep warm. Peel bell pepper and cut in strips. In a small saucepan, combine remaining marinade, bell pepper and tomatoes. Bring to a boil and simmer 5 minutes, stirring occasionally. Garnish chicken with basil leaves and serve with sauce. Makes 4 servings.

Stuffed Quail in Port

4 oven-ready quail
4 stalks celery, chopped
2 leeks, chopped
Fresh mushroom slices and fresh herb
sprigs to garnish

Marinade:
1/3 cup ruby port
2 tablespoons olive oil
1 tablespoon chopped fresh thyme
1 tablespoon chopped fresh oregano
1 tablespoon chopped fresh winter
savory
1 garlic clove, crushed
1/2 teaspoon salt
1/2 teaspoon black pepper

Stuffing:
1/4 cup thinly sliced shallots
6 ozs. button mushrooms
1 tablespoon chopped fresh parsley
1/2 teaspoon salt
1/2 teaspoon black pepper
4 slices bacon, chopped

Cut feet and wing tips off each quail. Split quails lengthwise, cutting through 1 side of backbone from neck to tail. Lay quails flat on a cutting board with breast side up. Press down firmly, breaking backbone, to flatten quails. Make a slit between legs through flap of skin. Insert legs and pull through to secure. Loosen skin at breast end of bird to incorporate stuffing. To prepare marinade, in a large bowl, combine all marinade ingredients until well blended. Immerse quail, turning quail in marinade to coat evenly. Cover and refrigerate 4 hours. To prepare stuffing, in a food processor fitted with a metal blade, process shallots, mushrooms, parsley, salt and pepper until finely chopped. Heat a large skillet. Fry bacon until fat runs. Add mushroom mixture and fry quickly, stirring occasionally, until all liquid has been absorbed. Let stand until cold. Insert stuffing under skin of quail. Brush with marinade. Prepare a hot barbecue. Cook quail over hot heat 10 minutes, turning once and basting with more marinade if necessary. Keep warm. Heat remaining marinade in a small saucepan. Add celery and leeks. Cook 2 to 3 minutes or until vegetables are tender. Arrange around quail. Garnish with mushroom slices and herb sprigs. Makes 4 servings.

Barbecued Trout in Leaves

4 trout, cleaned, or 8 (2-1/2-oz.) red
   mullet, cleaned
8 grape leaves
1 teaspoon arrowroot
Fresh fennel sprigs and bay leaves to
   garnish

Marinade:
1 tablespoon olive oil
1 tablespoon Seville orange juice
Shredded peel 1 Seville orange
1 garlic clove, crushed
6 cardamon pods, crushed
1/2 teaspoon salt
1/2 teaspoon black pepper
1 teaspoon Dijon-style mustard
2 bay leaves
1 tablespoon chopped fresh fennel

Rinse fish under running water. Pat dry
on paper towels. Score flesh on each
side of fish with a sharp knife. To prepare marinade, in a large bowl, combine all marinade ingredients until well
blended. Immerse fish in marinade,
turning fish to coat evenly. Cover and
refrigerate 1 hour. Remove fish from
marinade and loosely wrap each fish in
a grape leaf. Prepare a barbecue. Arrange fish on a rack in a grill pan. Cook
6 minutes, turning once. Unwrap fish.
Add juices from pan to remaining
marinade and blend with arrowroot.
Pour into a small saucepan and bring to
a boil, stirring constantly. Cook 1 minute. Pour sauce over fish and garnish
with fennel sprigs and bay leaves.
Makes 4 servings.

Barbecued Trout

8 trout
Fresh herb sprigs and lemon wedges to
   garnish

Marinade:
1/3 cup plain yogurt
1/2 teaspoon hot-pepper sauce
1/2 teaspoon cayenne pepper
1 tablespoon tomato paste
1/4 cup sherry
1/2 teaspoon salt
1/4 teaspoon black pepper
1 teaspoon superfine sugar
1 tablespoon plus 1 teaspoon chopped
   fresh basil leaves
2 teaspoons chopped fresh chives
2 teaspoons finely grated lemon peel

Wash and clean fish. Remove heads if desired. Dry well on paper towels. To prepare marinade, in a small bowl, combine all marinade ingredients until evenly blended. Pour into a large shallow dish. Add fish 1 at a time and turn fish gently in marinade to coat evenly. Cover and refrigerate 1 to 2 hours. Prepare a hot barbecue. Cook fish quickly over hot heat, turning once, 5 to 6 minutes or until crisp. Brush with more marinade if necessary. Garnish with herb sprigs and lemon wedges. Makes 4 servings.

Buttered Herb Sole Fillets

16 Dover sole fillets
1/2 cup unsalted butter
1 tablespoon plus 1 teaspoon chopped
   fresh tarragon
1 tablespoon plus 1 teaspoon all-purpose
   flour
2 tablespoons half and half
Fresh fennel sprigs to garnish

Marinade:
1 cup white wine
1 tablespoons chopped fresh fennel
1 Red Delicious apple, peeled, grated
2 teaspoons superfine sugar
1/2 teaspoon salt
1/2 teaspoon cayenne pepper

Wash fish. Pat dry on paper towels. To prepare marinade, in a shallow flameproof dish, combine all marinade ingredients until well blended. Add fish, turning fish in marinade to coat evenly. Cover and refrigerate 1 to 2 hours. In a small bowl, blend butter and tarragon. Lay fish flat on a cutting board. Spread 1/2 of each fish with herbed butter. Roll up firmly and secure each with a wooden pick. Arrange rolled fish in a large skillet. Cover and simmer 5 to 6 minutes or until fish is tender. Remove fish and keep warm. In a small bowl, blend flour and half and half. Strain marinade into flour and half and half, stirring well. Return to skillet. Bring to a boil and cook 1 minute. Garnish fish with fennel sprigs and serve with sauce. Makes 4 to 5 servings.

French Country Cod Steaks

4 (1-inch-thick) cod steaks
1 tablespoon butter, softened
1 tablespoon all-purpose flour
Fresh tarragon sprigs to garnish

Marinade:
1 red bell pepper
1 yellow bell pepper
16 black olives, pitted
4 tomatoes, peeled, seeded, sliced
2 zucchini, sliced
1 red onion, sliced
1 garlic clove, crushed
2 tablespoons olive oil
2/3 cup strong cider
1/2 teaspoon salt
1/2 teaspoon black pepper
1 teaspoon prepared mustard
1 tablespoon plus 1 teaspoon chopped
    fresh tarragon

Preheat broiler. To prepare marinade, place bell peppers on a baking sheet. Broil 10 minutes, turning occasionally, until skins are blistered and charred. Cool bell peppers. Peel and remove stalk and seeds. Cut in strips and place in a shallow baking dish. Stir in olives, tomatoes, zucchini, onion, garlic, olive oil, cider, salt, pepper, mustard and tarragon until well mixed. Immerse fish in marinade, turning fish to coat evenly. Cover and refrigerate 1 hour. Preheat oven to 400F (205C). Bake fish on a baking sheet in preheated oven 25 to 30 minutes or until tender. Remove bones and skin. Pour marinade into a small saucepan. In a small dish, blend butter and flour. Stir into marinade to thicken. Bring to a boil, then cook 2 minutes. Pour sauce over fish and garnish with tarragon sprigs. Makes 4 servings.

Honeyed Ginger Shrimp in Batter

8 jumbo shrimp with tails
Oil for deep frying
1 teaspoon arrowroot
Tangerine or satsuma wedges and fresh
    herb sprigs to garnish

Marinade:
1 tablespoon light soy sauce
1 tablespoon dry sherry
2 teaspoons finely grated tangerine or
    satsuma peel
1 tablespoon tangerine or satsuma juice
1 garlic clove, crushed
2 teaspoons honey
1/2 teaspoon black pepper

Batter:
3/4 cup all-purpose flour
1/4 teaspoon salt
1/4 teaspoon dry mustard powder
1/4 teaspoon black pepper
1 tablespoon plus 1 teaspoon olive oil
1/3 cup beer
2 egg whites

To prepare marinade, in a large bowl, combine all marinade ingredients until well mixed. Add shrimp, turning shrimp in marinade to coat evenly. Cover and refrigerate 2 hours. To prepare batter, in a large bowl, combine flour, salt, dry mustard and pepper. Make a well in center. Using a wooden spoon, mix in olive oil and beer to form a batter. Beat until smooth. Cover and refrigerate 30 minutes. Drain shrimp well. Stiffly whisk egg whites and fold into batter. Half-fill a deep saucepan with oil. Heat to 350F (175C). Hold shrimp by tails and dip into batter. Fry in oil 2 to 3 minutes or until golden brown. Drain on paper towels and keep warm. Blend arrowroot and marinade in a small saucepan. Bring to a boil, stirring constantly. Cook 30 seconds. Arrange 2 shrimp on each serving plate. Spoon a small amount of sauce on shrimp. Garnish with tangerine wedges and fresh herb sprigs. Makes 4 servings.

Mussels with Basil Sauce

32 fresh mussels
1/4 cup butter, softened
2 tablespoons all-purpose flour
2 tablespoons chopped fresh basil leaves
1/3 cup water
2 tablespoons half and half
Fresh bay leaves and pink peppercorns
  to garnish

Marinade:
3 tablespoons olive oil
1 tablespoon raspberry vinegar
1 tablespoon chopped fresh parsley
2 teaspoons pink peppercorns, crushed
1/2 teaspoon salt
1/2 teaspoon black pepper
1 teaspoon Dijon-style mustard

Scrub mussels thoroughly under running water, scraping shells clean with a small knife if necessary. Pull beards or thin strands from side of shells. In a stainless steel saucepan, heat mussels very gently, covered, until all shells have opened. Remove pan from heat. To prepare marinade, in a small bowl, combine all marinade ingredients until well blended. Stir into mussels and let stand 1 hour. Bring mussels to a boil and cook 1 minute. Discard any mussels that do not open. One at a time, remove empty side of mussel shell and arrange remainder in a shallow serving dish. In a small bowl, blend butter and flour. Stir in chopped basil. Whisk into marinade, add water and bring to a boil. Stir in half and half and pour sauce over mussels. Garnish with bay leaves and peppercorns. Makes 4 to 6 servings.

Salmon in Pastry

4 (4-oz.) salmon steaks, skinned, boned
6 ozs. oyster mushrooms
1/3 cup unsalted butter
4 sheets filo pastry
2 teaspoons arrowroot
1 tablespoon half and half
Fresh fennel sprigs, lemon wedges and
    pink peppercorns to garnish

Marinade:
2 teaspoons light-brown sugar
2 tablespoons rosé wine
2 tablespoons raspberry vinegar
2 teaspoons pink peppercorns, crushed
1 tablespoon plus 1 teaspoon chopped
    fresh fennel
1 tablespoon plus 1 teaspoon chopped
    fresh oregano

Arrange fish in a shallow dish. To prepare marinade, in a small bowl, combine all marinade ingredients until evenly mixed. Pour over fish, turning fish to coat evenly. Cover and refrigerate 1 hour. Reserve several mushrooms. Thinly slice remaining mushrooms. Melt 2 tablespoons of butter in a small saucepan. Saute sliced mushrooms in butter. Drain, reserve liquid and let stand until cold. Preheat oven to 400F (205C). Butter a baking sheet. Melt remaining butter. Brush each sheet of filo pastry with melted butter and fold in half. Drain fish well. Place 1 steak in center of each piece of folded pastry. Top each with mushroom slices and wrap up. Place on prepared baking sheet. Brush each parcel with remaining butter. Bake in preheated oven 15 minutes or until pastry is crisp and lightly browned. In a small saucepan, combine remaining marinade, mushroom liquid and arrowroot until blended. Bring to a boil and cook 1 minute. Stir in half and half. Garnish parcels with fennel sprigs, lemon wedges and pink peppercorns and serve with sauce. Makes 4 servings.

Seafood Kebabs

3/4 lb. monk fish (thick end)
3 flounder fillets
3 zucchini
1 small yellow bell pepper, seeded
12 large shrimp, peeled
Fresh bay leaves, lime wedges and fresh
   dill sprigs to garnish

Marinade:
1/4 teaspoon powdered saffron
Finely grated peel 1 lime
1 tablespoon fresh lime juice
1 tablespoon honey
1 teaspoon green peppercorns, crushed
2 tablespoons white vermouth
1/3 cup grapeseed oil
1/2 teaspoon salt
1/2 teaspoon black pepper
6 fresh bay leaves
1 tablespoon chopped fresh dill weed

To prepare marinade, in a large bowl, combine all marinade ingredients until well blended. Cut monk fish in bite-size pieces. Slice flounder fillets in thin strips. Cut zucchini and bell pepper in bite-size pieces. Stir fish, vegetables and shrimp into marinade, turning vegetables and fish carefully in marinade to coat evenly. Cover and refrigerate 1 hour. Soak 6 wooden skewers in cold water. Thread alternate pieces of fish, zucchini and bell pepper onto skewers. Remove bay leaves from marinade and attach a bay leaf at end of each skewer. Prepare a hot barbecue. Cook kebabs over hot heat 5 to 8 minutes, turning only once and brushing with more marinade as required. Garnish with bay leaves, lime wedges and dill sprigs. Makes 6 servings.

Spicy Scallops

12 scallops, cleaned
1/3 cup cider
2 tablespoons all-purpose flour
1 tablespoon butter, softened
2 teaspoons finely grated lemon peel
2 tablespoons fresh lemon juice
1 tablespoon chopped fresh dill weed
Toast triangles, fresh dill sprigs and
   lemon wedges to garnish

Marinade:
1/3 cup dairy sour cream
1/2 teaspoon ground cumin
1/2 teaspoon ground cinnamon
1/2 teaspoon turmeric
1 teaspoon grated gingerroot
2 teaspoons honey
1/2 teaspoon salt
1/2 teaspoon black pepper

In a medium-size saucepan, simmer scallops and cider 1 minute. To prepare marinade, in a medium-size bowl, combine all marinade ingredients until well blended. Using a slotted spoon, remove scallops from liquor. Cut each in half. Add to marinade, turning scallops to coat evenly. Cover and refrigerate 1 hour. Whisk flour and butter into scallop liquor in saucepan. Bring to a boil, whisking until sauce thickens. Stir in scallops, marinade, lemon peel and juice and dill. Simmer until mixture comes to a boil, stirring occasionally. Divide scallops between 6 shells or individual serving dishes. Garnish with toast triangles, dill sprigs and lemon wedges. Makes 6 servings.

Trout in Aspic

4 (8-oz.) trout, cleaned
1/3 cup mayonnaise
2 teaspoon tomato paste
2 tablespoons fresh lemon juice
2 (1/4-oz.) pkgs. gelatin
1 cucumber, very thinly sliced
Salt
Lemon wedges to garnish

Marinade:
1 red onion, sliced
1/2 cup chopped fennel bulb
2 bay leaves
2 tablespoons chopped fresh parsley
2/3 cup white wine
1/2 teaspoon salt
1/2 teaspoon black pepper

Thoroughly rinse trout under cold running water. Dry on paper towels. Arrange trout in a shallow baking dish so they are straight. To prepare marinade, in a medium-size bowl, combine all marinade ingredients until well blended. Pour marinade over trout. Cover and refrigerate 2 to 3 hours. Preheat oven to 375F (190C). Bake trout in preheated oven 15 to 20 minutes or until trout flakes easily. Let stand until cold. Remove trout from marinade. Preparing 1 trout at a time, carefully peel away skin and remove fins, leaving head and tail intact. Carefully remove top fillet of trout. Place bottom fillet on a serving plate. Using scissors, cut through center bone of bottom fillet at head and tail end. Lift off and remove with any remaining small bones. In a small bowl, mix mayonnaise and tomato paste. Spread bottom of fillets with mayonnaise mixture and replace top fillets. Strain marinade into a small bowl. Stir in lemon juice. In a small bowl, blend 3 tablespoons of marinade and gelatin. Set over a saucepan of hot water and stir until gelatin dissolves. Stir into remaining marinade and let stand until just beginning to thicken. Sprinkle cucumber slices with salt. Let stand 15 minutes and drain. Rinse under cold water and dry on paper towels. Brush each trout with marinade. Arrange overlapping cucumber slices to cover each trout from tail to head. Spoon marinade over trout to glaze each trout carefully. Refrigerate until set. Garnish with lemon wedges. Makes 4 servings.

Asparagus with Avocado Dressing

1 lb. fresh asparagus spears
1 ripe avocado
1 tablespoon plus 1 teaspoon chopped
   pistachio nuts or walnuts
Fresh fennel sprigs and orange segments
   to garnish

Marinade:
1/2 cup walnut oil
2 tablespoons fresh orange juice
2 teaspoons grated orange peel
2 teaspoons light-brown sugar
1/2 teaspoon salt
1/2 teaspoon black pepper
2 teaspoons Dijon-style mustard
2 tablespoons chopped fresh fennel

Trim asparagus. Using a sharp knife, peel each stem. In large shallow pan cook asparagus in boiling salted water 5 to 8 minutes or until tender. Drain and cool. To prepare marinade, in a small bowl, combine all marinade ingredients until well blended. Place asparagus in a shallow dish. Pour over marinade, turning asparagus in marinade to coat evenly. Cover and refrigerate 1 hour or until ready to serve. Arrange asparagus on 4 individiual serving plates. Peel and dice avocado. Carefully stir avocado and nuts into marinade. Spoon avocado and nut mixture over center of asparagus. Garnish with fennel, and orange segments. Makes 4 servings.

— Eggplant Filled Mushrooms with Basil —

8 large mushrooms
1 eggplant
1 garlic clove, crushed
1 (3-oz.) pkg. cream cheese
Salt and black pepper to taste
Fresh basil sprigs to garnish

Marinade:
3 tomatoes, peeled, seeded
1/4 cup olive oil
1/4 teaspoon salt
1/4 teaspoon black pepper
1 teaspoon sugar
Juice 1 orange
1 tablespoon plus 1 teaspoon chopped
    fresh basil

Remove stalks from mushrooms. To prepare marinade, in a food processor fitted with a metal blade, process stalks and all marinade ingredients until smooth. Spoon marinade into each mushroom and pour remainder into a small dish. Cover and refrigerate 1 hour. Meanwhile, preheat oven to 425F (220C). Bake eggplant in pre-heated oven 15 to 20 minutes or until skin is charred and flesh is tender. Cool and peel. Scrape out flesh into food processor fitted with a metal blade. Add garlic and cream cheese. Season to taste with salt and pepper. Process mixture until smooth. Place mushrooms on a baking sheet. Bake 5 minutes. Spoon eggplant mixture into each mushroom. Return to oven 5 to 8 minutes or until filling has set and mushrooms are tender. Garnish with basil sprigs. Makes 4 servings.

Crispy Coated Vegetables

8 large mushrooms, cut in half
2 zucchini, cut in 1/2-inch slices
1 cup Chinese snow peas or dwarf
  French green beans, ends removed
1 small fennel bulb, broken in bite-size
  pieces
1 cup cauliflower or broccoli floweretes
1 cup self-rising flour
1 egg
2/3 cup water
Oil for deep-frying
Lime wedges and fresh fennel sprigs to
  garnish

Marinade:
2 tablespoons plus 2 teaspoons chopped
  fresh basil
2 teaspoons finely grated lime peel
1 tablespoon fresh lime juice
1 teaspoon finely grated gingerroot
1 teaspoon superfine sugar
2 tablespoons olive oil
1/2 teaspoon salt
1/2 teaspoon black pepper

To prepare marinade, in a large bowl, combine all marinade ingredients until well blended. Add all vegetables to marinade, turning vegetables in marinade to coat evenly. Cover and refrigerate 1 hour or until ready to cook. To prepare batter, place flour in a medium-size bowl. Make a "well" in center. Add egg yolk and gradually stir in water. Beat until smooth. Stiffly whisk egg white and fold into batter just before using. Half-fill a deep saucepan with oil. Heat to 350F (175C). Dip 1 piece of vegetable at a time into batter to coat evenly, then place in oil. Fry about 12 pieces of vegetables at a time until lightly browned and crisp. Drain on paper towels. Garnish with lime and fennel sprigs. Makes 4 servings.

Curried Vegetables

1-1/4 cups cubed kohlrabbi
4 stalks celery, sliced
1/2 cup broccoli or cauliflower flowerets
2/3 cup cubed carrots
1-1/3 cups cubed potato or Jerusalem
    artichokes
1/2 cup all-purpose flour
1/4 cup butter
2/3 cup milk
1-1/4 cups vegetable stock
Fresh flat-leaf parsley sprigs to garnish

Marinade:
2 teaspoons cumin seeds
2 teaspoons coriander seeds
6 cardamon pods
2 teaspoons ground turmeric
2 teaspoons garam masala
1/2 teaspoon salt
1/2 teaspoon black pepper
1 garlic clove

To prepare marinade, place cumin, coriander seeds and seeds from cardamon pods into a pestle and mortar. Crush finely. Add turmeric, garam masala, salt, pepper and garlic. Work in pestle and mortar until evenly blended. In a large saucepan, cook all vegetables in boiling salted water 2 to 3 minutes until slightly tender. Drain stock from vegetables into a large measuring cup. In a large bowl, toss vegetables in marinade until evenly coated. Refrigerate 2 hours to marinate. To prepare sauce, in a medium-size saucepan, combine flour, butter, milk and vegetable stock. Bring to a boil, whisking until sauce thickens. Gently stir in vegetables. Bring to a boil, cover and simmer 20 minutes or until vegetables are tender. Garnish with parsley sprigs. Makes 4 servings.

Dill Cucumber Frais

1 medium-size cucumber
2/3 cup water
1 cup dairy sour cream
Fresh dill sprigs and chive flowers to
  garnish

Marinade:
1 tablespoon plus 1 teaspoon chopped
  fresh tarragon
1 tablespoon plus 1 teaspoon chopped
  fresh dill
1 tablespoon plus 1 teaspoon snipped
  fresh chives
1/2 teaspoon salt
1/2 teaspoon black pepper
1/2 teaspoon dry mustard powder
2 tablespoon red vermouth

Using a zester, remove thin strips of cucumber peel to make a ridge effect. Cut cucumber in half lengthwise. Scoop out seeds and cut in 1/2-inch slices. Bring water to a boil in medium-size saucepan. Cook cucumber 1 minute and drain. To prepare marinade, in a medium-size bowl, combine all marinade ingredients until well blended. Add cucumber, turning cucumber gently in marinade to coat. Cover and refrigerate 2 hours. Just before serving, gently stir in sour cream until evenly mixed. Garnish with dill sprigs and chive flowers. Makes 4 servings.

Marinated Bell Peppers

2 green bell peppers
2 yellow bell peppers
2 red bell peppers
Fresh herb sprigs to garnish

Marinade:
1/3 cup almond oil
1 tablespoon cider vinegar
1 tablespoon honey
1/2 teaspoon salt
1/2 teaspoon black pepper
1 teaspoon Dijon-style mustard
1 teaspoon tomato paste
2 teaspoons snipped fresh chives
2 teaspoons chopped fresh parsley
2 teaspoons chopped fresh marjoram
2 teaspoons chopped fresh winter savory
1 garlic clove
1 teaspoon sugar

Preheat oven to 425F (220C). Place bell peppers on a baking sheet. Bake in preheated oven 15 to 20 minutes or until skins are black and charred and bell peppers are tender. Plunge bell peppers into cold water to cool quickly, then drain. Peel, remove stalks and seeds. Cut each pepper in 1/2-inch strips and arrange in a shallow serving dish. To prepare marinade, in a small bowl, combine all marinade ingredients until well blended. Pour marinade over bell peppers. Cover and refrigerate 1 to 2 hours. Garnish with herb sprigs. Makes 4 servings.

Marinated Stuffed Leaves

8 small spinach leaves
8 small Chinese cabbage leaves
8 small radichio leaves
1 (8-oz.) pkg. cream cheese, softened
1 garlic clove, crushed
2 tablespoons chopped fresh parsley
1 yellow bell pepper
Fresh herb sprigs and shredded orange
    peel to garnish

Marinade:
1 teaspoon finely grated orange peel
1 tablespoon fresh orange juice
1/3 cup olive oil
1 tablespoon chopped fresh marjoram
1/2 teaspoon salt
1/2 teaspoon black pepper
1 teaspoon Dijon-style mustard
1 teaspoon superfine sugar

Plunge spinach leaves into boiling water 30 seconds. Using a slotted spoon, remove leaves and refresh in cold water. Drain well. Repeat with Chinese and radichio leaves, keeping each separate. To prepare marinade, in a large bowl, combine all marinade ingredients until well blended. Pour 1/3 of marinade into a separate medium-size bowl. Add radichio leaves to separate bowl, turning leaves in to marinade to coat. Place spinach and Chinese leaves in remaining marinade, turning leaves to coat evenly. Cover and refrigerate 2 hours. To prepare filling, in a small bowl, beat cream cheese, garlic and parsley until evenly blended. Cover and refrigerate until needed. Preheat oven to 425F (220C). Bake bell pepper on a baking sheet in preheated oven 15 to 20 minutes or until skin is charred. Peel bell pepper and remove stalk and seeds. In a food processor fitted with a metal blade, process bell pepper until smooth. Drain leaves, reserving marinade. Spread out 1 leaf at a time flat on a cutting board. Place 1 teaspoonful of cream cheese mixture in center, fold in edges and roll up firmly. Repeat with remaining leaves and cream cheese mixture. Place on a serving dish. Combine bell pepper and remaining marinade. Pour around leaves in dish. Garnish with herb sprigs and orange peel. Makes 4 servings.

Mixed Vegetable Kebabs

1 (12-oz.) eggplant, cut in bite-size pieces
Salt
1 small red bell pepper, seeded, cut in
   3/4-inch squares
1 small yellow bell pepper, seeded, cut
   in 3/4-inch squares
4 small zucchini, trimmed, cut in
   1/2-inch slices
8 shallots, each cut in 4 pieces
16 button mushrooms
16 cherry tomatoes
Fresh oregano sprigs to garnish

Marinade:
1/3 cup olive oil
1 tablespoon raspberry vinegar
1/2 teaspoon black pepper
1/2 teaspoon salt
1 teaspoon dry mustard powder
1 tablespoon light-brown sugar
1 tablespoon chopped fresh oregano
1 tablespoon chopped fresh parsley

Soak 8 wooden skewers in cold water. To prepare marinade, in a large bowl, combine all marinade ingredients until well blended. Place eggplant in a colander or sieve set over a bowl. Sprinkle with salt. Cover with a plate to weight and let stand 30 minutes. Rinse eggplant thoroughly to remove salt, then press out excess water. Add all vegetables to marinade, turning vegetables carefully to coat completely. Cover and refrigerate 1 hour. Meanwhile, prepare a barbecue. Thread a mixture of vegetables onto presoaked skewers. Cook 3 to 5 minutes or until vegetables are just tender, brushing with marinade. Garnish with oregano. Makes 8 servings.

Ratatouille

1 small eggplant, thinly sliced
Salt
1/3 cup olive oil
1 small red bell pepper, seeded,
   thinly sliced
1 small yellow bell pepper, seeded,
   thinly sliced
2 medium-size onions, thinly sliced
3 small zucchini, thinly sliced
3 medium-size tomatoes, peeled, seeded,
   thinly sliced
Fresh herb sprigs to garnish

Marinade:
2 tablespoons red wine
1 garlic clove
2 tablespoons chopped fresh cilantro
2 tablespoons chopped fresh basil
2 tablespoons chopped fresh parsley
1 teaspoon Dijon-style mustard
1/2 teaspoon salt
1/2 teaspoon black pepper

Arrange eggplant in a sieve set over a bowl, sprinkling between layers with salt. Cover with a plate to weight and let stand 30 minutes. Rinse under cold running water. Dry on paper towels. Heat olive oil in a large skillet. Saute eggplant, peppers, onions and zucchini, stirring occasionally, 4 to 5 minutes or until vegetables are almost tender. Add tomatoes. Cook 3 to 4 minutes or until vegetables are tender. To prepare marinade, in a large bowl, combine all marinade ingredients until well blended. Add vegetables, turning vegetables in marinade to completely coat. Let stand until cold. Garnish with herb sprigs. Makes 6 servings.

Spiced Okra

3/4 lb. okra, washed, ends removed
4 medium-size tomatoes, peeled, seeded,
  chopped
2/3 cup water
1/2 cup plain yogurt
Fresh flat-leaf parsley sprigs to garnish

Marinade:
1 red chili pepper, seeded, chopped
1 onion, finely chopped
1 garlic clove, crushed
1 teaspoon ground cumin
1 teaspoon ground coriander
1/2 teaspoon salt
1/2 teaspoon black pepper
1 teaspoon sugar
2 tablespoons olive oil

To prepare marinade, in a large bowl, combine all marinade ingredients until well blended. Add okra to marinade, turning okra carefully until evenly coated. Cover and refrigerate 1 hour. In a large saucepan, bring tomatoes and water to a boil. Add okra and marinade. Bring to a boil, stirring carefully, then cover and simmer 15 to 20 minutes or until okra is tender. Remove okra with a slotted spoon and arrange on a serving plate. Drain tomato mixture. Gently combine yogurt and tomato mixture. Spoon tomato mixture onto spiced okra. Garnish with parsley sprigs and serve hot or cold. Makes 4 to 6 servings.

Brandied Fruit Crepes

1 cup all-purpose flour
2/3 cup milk
2/3 cup water
1 egg
1/4 cup apricot brandy
Butter or oil for frying
Fresh mint leaves or tiny flowers to
   decorate

Marinated Fruit:
3/4 cup superfine sugar
1-1/4 cups water
4 strips lemon peel
4 ozs. kumquats
3 medium-size nectarines, sliced

To prepare marinated fruit, in a large saucepan, simmer sugar, water and lemon peel, stirring constantly, until sugar has dissolved. Add kumquats. Bring to a boil. Cover and simmer 5 minutes or until kumquats are tender. Pour kumquats into a large bowl. Add nectarines and let stand until cold.

Meanwhile, to prepare crepes, place flour in a large bowl. In a medium-size bowl, whisk milk, water and egg until well blended. Make a "well" in center of flour. Add 1/2 of milk mixture and beat well with a wooden spoon. Add remaining milk mixture, beating well. Melt enough butter to lightly grease a small crepe pan or skillet. Pour in enough batter to just thinly coat bottom of pan. Swirl pan to spread batter. Cook until underside is lightly brown, about 1 minute. Using a small knife, turn crepe over. Cook until crepe moves freely in pan. Place on a plate covered with paper towels. Repeat with remaining batter. Cover and keep warm. Strain syrup from fruit into a small saucepan. Boil 3 to 4 minutes or until thick and syrupy. Cool slightly, stir in brandy and pour over fruit. Fold crepes in quarters. Serve with kumquats, nectarines and syrup. Decorate with mint leaves. Makes 4 servings.

Fig & Port Ice Cream

1/2 cup superfine sugar
2/3 cup ruby port
1 (2-inch) piece cinnamon stick
6 fresh figs
1 tablespoon plus 1 teaspoon fresh lime
    juice
1-1/4 cups whipping cream
Crisp ice cream cups, if desired
Fresh fig slices and fresh mint leaves to
    decorate

In a medium-size saucepan, combine sugar and port. Simmer, stirring occasionally, until sugar has melted. Bring to a boil and add cinnamon and 6 figs. Cover and simmer 5 minutes. Let stand until completely cold. In a food processor fitted with a metal blade, process figs and liquid until smooth. Pour mixture into a sieve set over a bowl. Press mixture through sieve using a wooden spoon. Stir in lime juice. In a small bowl, whip cream until thick. Fold into fig puree until evenly blended. Pour mixture into a container. Cover and freeze 1 to 2 hours or until mixture is almost frozen but still soft. Return mixture to food processor. Process until thick and smooth. Return to container and freeze until firm. If desired, serve in crisp ice cream cups. Decorate with fig slices and mint. Makes 6 servings.

Gingered Melon Cup

2 grapefruit, cut in half
1 Ogen melon
1 cup pitted fresh sweet cherries
1 cup seedless purple grapes
Fresh ginger mint sprigs and strawberry
  slices to decorate

Marinade:
2/3 cup ginger wine
1/4 cup superfine sugar
1 tablespoon plus 2 teaspoons chopped
  fresh ginger mint
1 tablespoon plus 1 teaspoon chopped
  preserved ginger in heavy syrup

Remove grapefruit segments and place in a large bowl. Reserve grapefruit shells. Using a melon baller, scoop balls from melon. Add to grapefruit in bowl. Reserve melon shells. Combine grapefruit segments, melon balls, cherries and grapes. To prepare marinade, in a small bowl, combine all marinade ingredients until well blended. Pour marinade over fruit, turning fruit carefully to coat evenly. Cover and refrigerate until needed. Using small sharp scissors, cut edge of each grapefruit and melon shell in a zig-zag. Fill each shell with fruit and marinade mixture. Decorate with ginger mint and strawberries. Makes 6 servings.

Jewelled Fruit Mold

2 cups red grape juice
2 cups white grape juice
2 (1/4-oz.) pkgs. gelatin (6 teaspoons)
1/3 cup water
Strawberry and star fruit slices and fresh
    mint sprigs to decorate.

Marinated Fruit:
1 tablespoon plus 1 teaspoon orange
    flower water or Cointreau
1 tablespoon plus 1 teaspoon rose water
    or kirsch
2 tablespoons plus 2 teaspoons powdered
    sugar
1 star fruit, sliced
1 cup seedless white grapes
1 cup fresh cherries, pitted
1 cup fresh strawberries, sliced

Pour red and white grape juice into separate medium-size bowls. In a small bowl, stir gelatin into water. Set bowl over a saucepan of hot water and stir until gelatin is dissolved. Stir 1/2 of gelatin into each bowl of grape juice.

To prepare marinated fruit, pour orange flower water and rose water onto separate plates. Stir 1/2 of powdered sugar into each. Add star fruit and grapes to orange flower water mixture and cherries and strawberries to rose water mixture, turning fruit carefully to coat evenly. Cover and let stand 30 minutes. Pour 1/2 inch of white juice into a 6-cup mold or 8 individual molds. Refrigerate until white juice begins to set. Arrange 1/3 of star fruit and grapes over set white juice. Spoon enough white juice over fruit to cover. Refrigerate until white juice begins to set. Arrange 1/3 of cherries and strawberries over set white juice. Cover with red juice and refrigerate until set. Repeat this layering until all fruit and juices have been used. Stir any remaining marinade into last layer of red and white juice. Refrigerate 1 hour until set. Dip mold into hand-hot water 1 to 2 seconds and invert onto a serving plate. Decorate with strawberries, star fruit and mint sprigs. Makes 8 servings.

Fruit Cheese Dessert

1/4 cup Marsala wine
1/4 teaspoon ground mace
1 cup mixed glacé fruits, chopped
1-1/2 cups riccotta cheese or cream
   cheese
1 tablespoon plus 1 teaspoon superfine
   sugar
2 eggs, separated
2 teaspoons grated lemon peel
2/3 cup whipping cream
Fresh or glacé fruit and fresh mint
   sprigs to decorate

In a small bowl, combine wine, mace and glace fruits until well blended. Cover and let stand several hours. In a medium-size bowl, beat riccotta cheese, sugar, egg yolks and lemon peel with a wooden spoon until smooth. Stir in marinated fruit until well mixed. Whisk egg whites. Whip cream in a small bowl until soft peaks form. Using a spatula or metal spoon, alternately fold egg whites and whipped cream into cheese and fruit mixture. Spoon mixture into 6 small dessert dishes. Refrigerate 1 hour before serving. Decorate top of each dessert with fruit and mint sprigs. Makes 6 servings.

Fruits in Wine

2/3 cup sweet white wine
2/3 cup sweet red wine
1-1/4 cups water
1/4 cup superfine sugar
4 strips lemon peel
2 teaspoon ground mace
6 fresh lemon balm leaves
6 ripe apricots
1/4 cup light-brown sugar
1 (2-inch) piece cinnamon stick
4 whole cloves
4 strips orange peel
6 fresh mint leaves
6 red plums
Fresh mint and lemon balm leaves and
   orange twists to decorate

Pour white and red wine into separate saucepans, each with 1/2 of water. Stir sugar, lemon peel, mace and lemon balm leaves into white wine. Bring to a boil. Add apricots, cover and simmer 5 to 8 minutes or until apricots are tender. Carefully spoon apricots into a small bowl. Cover with marinade so apricots are completely immersed. Refrigerate until cold. Meanwhile, stir brown sugar, cinnamon, cloves, orange peel and mint leaves into red wine. Bring to a boil. Add plums, cover and simmer 8 to 10 minutes or until plums are tender. Carefully spoon plums into a small bowl. Cover with marinade so plums are completely immersed. Refrigerate until cold. Remove apricots and plums from syrup. Place on separate serving plates. Strain each marinade back into separate saucepans and boil rapidly 1 to 2 minutes or until syrupy. Pour red syrup over plums and white syrup over apricots. Refrigerate until cold. Decorate with mint and lemon leaves and orange twists. Makes 3 servings.

Mixed Fruit Kebabs

1 tablespoon plus 1 teaspoon dark rum
  or sherry
1/4 cup superfine sugar
1/2 fresh pineapple
2 oranges
2 nectarines, sliced
24 cherries, pitted
2 bananas, sliced
2 teaspoons fresh lemon juice
2 teaspoons ground cinnamon
2/3 cup whipping cream
Fresh mint leaves and orange slices to
  decorate

In a large bowl, combine rum and 1/2 of sugar. Cut out flesh from pineapple shell, allowing any juice to fall into rum mixture. Cut flesh in bite-sized pieces. Stir into rum mixture. Using a sharp knife, cut orange peel away from flesh, including all white pith. Cut out each orange segment, allowing juice to fall into rum mixture. Add orange segments, nectarine slices and cherries to rum mixture. Toss banana slices in lemon juice. Add to rum mixture, turning fruit carefully in marinade to coat evenly. Cover and let stand 15 minutes. Mix remaining sugar and cinnamon on a flat plate. Thread 6 thin wooden skewers with a mixture of fruit. Roll each kebab in cinnamon-sugar mixture to coat evenly. Whip cream in a small bowl until thick. Carefully fold in remaining marinade juices until well blended. Prepare a hot barbecue, Cook fruit kebabs, turning once, over hot heat 2 to 3 minutes or until hot and tinged with brown. Serve with whipped cream. Decorate with mint leaves and orange slices. Makes 6 servings.

Mixed Fruit Tarts

1/3 cup unsalted butter, cubed
1 cup all-purpose flour
1 tablespoon plus 2 teaspoons superfine
　sugar
1 egg yolk
1/2 (8-oz.) pkg. cream cheese
2/3 cup plain yogurt
1 teaspoon arrowroot

Marinated Fruit:
2 tablespoons plus 2 teaspoons grenadine
　syrup
2 tablespoons plus 2 teaspoons sweet
　white wine or cider
2 tablespoons fresh chopped apple mint
2 fresh figs, sliced
2 tablespoons plus 2 teaspoons black
　currants
2/3 cup seedless white grapes
1 fresh peach, sliced

To prepare pastry, in a medium-size bowl, cut butter into flour and rub in finely with fingers. Stir in sugar and egg yolk with a fork and mix to a soft dough. Wrap in plastic wrap and refrigerate 30 minutes. To prepare marinated fruit, in a small bowl, combine grenadine syrup, wine and mint. Add fig, black currants, grapes and peach, turning fruit carefully in marinade to coat evenly. Cover and refrigerate until chilled. Preheat oven to 375F (190C). On a floured flat surface, roll out pastry thinly. Line 8 individual brioche molds or tart pans with pastry. Prick pastry with a fork and refrigerate until firm. Place molds on a baking sheet. Bake in preheated oven 8 to 10 minutes or until pastry is light golden in color. Cool in molds 5 minutes, then turn out onto a wire rack. In a small bowl, combine cream cheese and yogurt. Strain marinade from fruit into a small saucepan and blend in arrowroot. Bring to a boil, stirring constantly. Cook 30 seconds or until thick, then cool. Fill each tartlet with cream cheese and marinated fruit. Glaze with thickened marinade. Makes 8 servings.

Rose Petal Pavlovas

3 egg whites
1 cup superfine sugar
1 tablespoon plus 1 teaspoon rose water
1 teaspoon raspberry vinegar
1 teaspoon cornstarch
Rose pink food coloring
1-1/4 cups whipping cream
1/2 cup plain yogurt
Rose petals and fresh mint sprigs to
  decorate

Marinated Fruit:
1 tablespoon plus 1 teaspoon rose water
1 tablespoon plus 1 teaspoon rose wine
2 tablespoons plus 2 teaspoons powdered
  sugar
2 tablespoons plus 2 teaspoons rose
  petals
2/3 cup fresh raspberries
2/3 cup fresh strawberries, sliced
1 cup red currants or cherries

Preheat oven to 250F (120C). Line 2 baking sheets with parchment paper. To prepare pavlovas, in a small bowl, whisk egg white until stiff. Add sugar a little at a time, whisking well after each addition, until thick. In a small bowl, combine rose water, vinegar, cornstarch and a drop of food coloring until evenly blended. Add to meringue, whisking until thick and glossy. Spoon 12 spoonfuls of meringue onto prepared baking sheets. Bake in preheated oven 45 minutes. Turn oven heat off and let stand until cold. To prepare marinated fruit, in a small bowl, combine rose water, wine, powdered sugar and rose petals. Add raspberries, strawberries and red currants, turning fruit carefully in marinade to coat evenly. Cover and refrigerate 30 minutes. Whip cream in a small bowl until thick. Add yogurt and strain in marinade liquid, folding in carefully until just mixed. Arrange pavlovas on a serving plate. Spoon cream mixture onto each. Top with mixed fruit and decorate with rose petals and mint sprigs. Makes 12 servings.

Tipsy Fruit Cloud

1/2 cup dairy sour cream
1/2 cup whipping cream
Fresh mint or lemon leaves and fresh
    fruit to decorate

Marinated Fruit:
1 tablespoon dark rum
1 tablespoon kirsch
1 tablespoon peach brandy
1/2 cup powdered sugar
2 teaspoons finely grated orange peel
2 kiwifruit, peeled, cubed
2 peaches, peeled, cubed
1/2 pineapple, cubed
1 cup fresh strawberries, cut in half

In a large bowl, combine rum, kirsch, brandy, powdered sugar and orange peel. Add all fruit to marinade, turning carefully to coat evenly. Cover and refrigerate 1 to 2 hours. In a small bowl, whip sour cream and whipping cream until thick. Strain mixed fruit and carefully fold fruit into cream mixture. Spoon fruit mixture into 6 glasses. Decorate with mint leaves and top with fresh fruit. Makes 6 servings.

INDEX